I0413539

Utility and Recognition of Lines and Linear Patterns on Electronic Displays Depicting Aeronautical Charting Information

DOT/FAA/AR-09/01

DOT-VNTSC-FAA-09-03

Air Traffic Organization Operations Planning

Human Factors Research and Engineering Group

Washington, DC 20591

Divya C. Chandra

U.S. Department of Transportation

Research and Innovative Technology Administration

John A. Volpe National Transportation Systems Center

Cambridge, MA 02142

January 2009

REPORT DOCUMENTATION PAGE

Form Approved
OMB No. 0704-0188

1. AGENCY USE ONLY (Leave blank)	2. REPORT DATE	3. REPORT TYPE AND DATES COVERED
	January 2009	

4. TITLE AND SUBTITLE	5. FUNDING NUMBERS
Utility and Recognition of Lines and Linear Patterns on Electronic Displays Depicting Aeronautical Charting Information	FA6Y/ED305
	FA6YC1/ED8RX and FD8RX
6. AUTHOR(S) Divya C. Chandra	

7. PERFORMING ORGANIZATION NAME(S) AND ADDRESS(ES)	8. PERFORMING ORGANIZATION REPORT NUMBER
U.S. Department of Transportation John A. Volpe National Transportation Systems Center Research and Innovative Technology Administration Cambridge, MA 02142-1093	DOT-VNTSC-FAA-09-03

9. SPONSORING/MONITORING AGENCY NAME(S) AND ADDRESS(ES)	10. SPONSORING/MONITORING AGENCY REPORT NUMBER
U.S. Department of Transportation Federal Aviation Administration Air Traffic Organization Operations Planning Human Factors Research and Engineering Group 800 Independence Avenue, SW Washington, D.C. 20591 Program Manager: Dr. Tom McCloy	DOT/FAA/AR-09/01

11. SUPPLEMENTARY NOTES

12a. DISTRIBUTION/AVAILABILITY STATEMENT	12b. DISTRIBUTION CODE
This document is available to the public through the National Technical Information Service, Springfield, VA 22161	

13. ABSTRACT (Maximum 200 words)

This report describes a study conducted to explore the utility and recognition of lines and linear patterns on electronic displays depicting aeronautical charting information. The study gathered data from a large number of pilots who conduct all types of flight operations. Lines and linear patterns that were useful to different pilot groups were identified based on pilot qualifications, types of flight operations, and typical flight length. Pilots were also asked to identify nine test linear patterns in isolation. This task was difficult, but some linear patterns were more recognizable than others. The tested lines and linear patterns will be considered in the development of an updated SAE International Aerospace Recommended Practices (ARP) document on Electronic Aeronautical Symbols (ARP 5289A). The Federal Aviation Administration or the International Civil Aviation Organization may choose to adopt this industry document by reference at a later date. Note that this research applies to any electronic display that shows the lines and linear patterns tested in this study, regardless of the intended function of the display.

14. SUBJECT TERM	15. NUMBER OF PAGES
Electronic displays, aeronautical charts, symbology, moving map displays, charting information, symbols, lines, linear patterns	81
	16. PRICE CODE

17. SECURITY CLASSIFICATION OF REPORT	18. SECURITY CLASSIFICATION OF THIS PAGE	19. SECURITY CLASSIFICATION OF ABSTRACT	20. LIMITATION OF ABSTRACT
Unclassified	Unclassified	Unclassified	

PREFACE

This report was prepared by the Behavioral Safety Research and Demonstration Division at the United States Department of Transportation Volpe National Transportation Systems Center. It was completed with funding from the FAA Human Factors Research and Engineering Group (AJP-61) in support of the Aircraft Certification Service Avionics Branch (AIR-130) and the Technical Programs and Continued Airworthiness Branch (AIR-120). I would like to thank the FAA program manager, Tom McCloy, as well as the FAA technical sponsor, Colleen Donovan, for their assistance with this project. I would also like to thank the members of the SAE International G-10 Aeronautical Charting Committee, who invested their expertise and time to make this study more valuable. In addition, I thank the International Federation of Airline Pilots' Associations (IFALPA), the National Business Aviation Association (NBAA), the Aircraft Owners and Pilots Association (AOPA), and the Air Force Flight Standards Agency for their assistance in recruiting participants. Particular thanks go to the many pilots who donated their time and input for the study. Finally, I would like to thank the Volpe Center staff who helped with the study: Michelle Yeh for assistance with the initial data analysis, Michael Zuschlag for assistance with the final data analysis, Rachel Selgrade and Catherine Guthy for assistance with the data processing and analysis, and Raquel Rodriguez for assistance with distributing the surveys.

The views expressed herein are those of the author and do not necessarily reflect the views of the Volpe National Transportation Systems Center, the Research and Innovative Technology Administration, or the United States Department of Transportation.

Feedback on this document may be sent to Divya Chandra (Divya.Chandra@volpe.dot.gov). Further information on this research effort can be found at http://www.volpe.dot.gov/hf.

METRIC/ENGLISH CONVERSION FACTORS

ENGLISH TO METRIC

LENGTH (APPROXIMATE)
1 inch (in) = 2.5 centimeters (cm)
1 foot (ft) = 30 centimeters (cm)
1 yard (yd) = 0.9 meter (m)
1 mile (mi) = 1.6 kilometers (km)

AREA (APPROXIMATE)
1 square inch (sq in, in²) = 6.5 square centimeters (cm²)
1 square foot (sq ft, ft²) = 0.09 square meter (m²)
1 square yard (sq yd, yd²) = 0.8 square meter (m²)
1 square mile (sq mi, mi²) = 2.6 square kilometers (km²)
1 acre = 0.4 hectare (he) = 4,000 square meters (m²)

MASS - WEIGHT (APPROXIMATE)
1 ounce (oz) = 28 grams (gm)
1 pound (lb) = 0.45 kilogram (kg)
1 short ton = 2,000 pounds (lb) = 0.9 tonne (t)

VOLUME (APPROXIMATE)
1 teaspoon (tsp) = 5 milliliters (ml)
1 tablespoon (tbsp) = 15 milliliters (ml)
1 fluid ounce (fl oz) = 30 milliliters (ml)
1 cup (c) = 0.24 liter (l)
1 pint (pt) = 0.47 liter (l)
1 quart (qt) = 0.96 liter (l)
1 gallon (gal) = 3.8 liters (l)
1 cubic foot (cu ft, ft³) = 0.03 cubic meter (m³)
1 cubic yard (cu yd, yd³) = 0.76 cubic meter (m³)

TEMPERATURE (EXACT)
[(x-32)(5/9)] °F = y °C

METRIC TO ENGLISH

LENGTH (APPROXIMATE)
1 millimeter (mm) = 0.04 inch (in)
1 centimeter (cm) = 0.4 inch (in)
1 meter (m) = 3.3 feet (ft)
1 meter (m) = 1.1 yards (yd)
1 kilometer (km) = 0.6 mile (mi)

AREA (APPROXIMATE)
1 square centimeter (cm²) = 0.16 square inch (sq in, in²)
1 square meter (m²) = 1.2 square yards (sq yd, yd²)
1 square kilometer (km²) = 0.4 square mile (sq mi, mi²)
10,000 square meters (m²) = 1 hectare (ha) = 2.5 acres

MASS - WEIGHT (APPROXIMATE)
1 gram (gm) = 0.036 ounce (oz)
1 kilogram (kg) = 2.2 pounds (lb)
1 tonne (t) = 1,000 kilograms (kg) = 1.1 short tons

VOLUME (APPROXIMATE)
1 milliliter (ml) = 0.03 fluid ounce (fl oz)
1 liter (l) = 2.1 pints (pt)
1 liter (l) = 1.06 quarts (qt)
1 liter (l) = 0.26 gallon (gal)
1 cubic meter (m³) = 36 cubic feet (cu ft, ft³)
1 cubic meter (m³) = 1.3 cubic yards (cu yd, yd³)

TEMPERATURE (EXACT)
[(9/5) y + 32] °C = x °F

QUICK INCH - CENTIMETER LENGTH CONVERSION

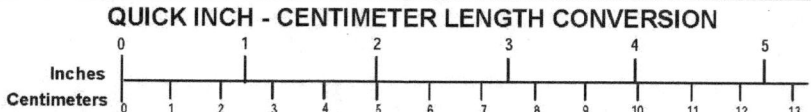

QUICK FAHRENHEIT - CELSIUS TEMPERATURE CONVERSION

°F	-40°	-22°	-4°	14°	32°	50°	68°	86°	104°	122°	140°	158°	176°	194°	212°
°C	-40°	-30°	-20°	-10°	0°	10°	20°	30°	40°	50°	60°	70°	80°	90°	100°

For more exact and or other conversion factors, see NIST Miscellaneous Publication 286, Units of Weights and Measures. Price $2.50
SD Catalog No. C13 10286   Updated 6/17/98

Table of Contents

List of Figures

List of Tables

Executive Summary

This report describes a study conducted to explore the utility and recognition of lines and linear patterns on electronic displays that depict aeronautical charting information. The goal of this research is to support the development of recommendations for more standardized and consistent lines and linear patterns on these displays. The study includes data from a large number of active pilots (273) who conduct all types of flight operations. This research was conducted with funding and technical assistance from the Federal Aviation Administration (FAA).

The main goals of the current study were to: (1) identify which lines and linear patterns should have specific recommendations, and which could be left to the manufacturer's discretion, and (2) identify whether there are some linear patterns that are currently well recognized and should be recommended for use as is, in order to aid pilots who already are familiar with them and to prevent future development of conflicting patterns.

The study consisted of three parts. First, pilots were asked to sort the names of 65 types of lines and linear patterns into three categories: Very Useful, Recognize and Use on Occasion, and Do Not Use/Do Not Recognize. The results of this task identified items that were useful to different pilot groups based on qualifications, types of flight operations, and typical flight length. The most broadly useful items were Controlled Airspace boundaries (e.g., Class B, C, and D) and Special Use Airspace boundaries (e.g., Restricted or Prohibited). Some items were more useful to pilots who conduct visual flight operations (e.g., roads and city patterns), while others were useful for instrument operations (e.g., missed approach procedure track and missed approach procedure holding pattern).

In the second part of the study, pilots were asked to identify nine test linear patterns that were expected by subject matter experts to be fairly recognizable. The patterns were shown in isolation, without color or other contextual clues that would normally be available, such as size and/or position on the display. Results of this task showed that identifying the linear patterns was difficult without context. Still, some linear patterns, such as the Special Use Airspace boundary, were more recognizable than others, such as the Air Route Traffic Control Center or Communications boundary.

Finally, in the third part of the study, pilots were asked to rate the importance of lines, the difficulty of interpreting lines on paper charts, and the difficulty of interpreting lines on electronic charts and map displays. Pilots were also asked to provide additional comments on the topic in general. The ratings indicated that pilots who report flying private operations considered line information to be more important than pilots who report flying air transport operations. Additionally, the ratings and comments suggested that line information was easier to interpret on electronic displays than paper charts. This is likely due to the fact that most electronic displays provide less information to the pilot than paper aeronautical charts, and they can be de-cluttered as well. Electronic displays can contain less information than paper charts because they are generally intended to be used in *conjunction* with paper charts.

The results of this research are expected to be of use to the FAA or International Civil Aviation Organization, who may choose to reference this report in support of their recommendations at a later date. This research will also be considered by SAE International in developing industry recommendations. This research is also expected to be of use to individual manufacturers who develop and/or depict lines and linear patterns for electronic displays of aeronautical charting information. Note that this research effort is independent of the type of electronic display and the results are applicable regardless of the display's intended function.

Acronyms

ADIZ	Air Defense Identification Zone
ANOVA	Analysis of Variance
ARP	Aerospace Recommended Practice
ARSA	Airport Radar Service Area
ARTCC	Air Route Traffic Control Center
ATM	Air Transportation Management
ATP	Air Transport Pilot
ATZ	Air Traffic Zone
CAA	Civil Aviation Authority
CNS	Communications Navigations and Surveillance
CTA/CTL	Control Area
CTZ/CTR	Control Zone
EFB	Electronic Flight Bag
FAA	Federal Aviation Administration
FIR	Flight Information Region
FMS	Flight Management System
HPZ	Helicopter Protected Zone
HTZ	Helicopter Traffic Zone
ICAO	International Civil Aviation Organization
IFR	Instrument Flight Rules
ILS	Instrument Landing System
MATZ	Military Air Traffic Zone
MCTR	Military Control Zone
MOA	Military Operations Area
NACO	National Aeronautical Charting Office
NDB	Non-Directional Beacon
NM	Nautical mile
OCA	Oceanic Control Area
PCA	Positive Control Area
QFE/QNH	Altimeter Setting Regions
RTCA	Organization formerly known as Radio Technical Commission for Aeronautics
RVSM	Reduced Vertical Separation Minima
STZ	Special Rules Area/Zone

SUA	Special Use Airspace
TCA/TMA	Terminal Control Area
TFR	Temporary Flight Restriction Area
TIA	Traffic Information Area/Zone
TRSA	Terminal Radar Service Area
UCA/UTA	Upper Control Area
UFIR	Upper Flight Information Region
US	United States
VFR	Visual Flight Rules

1 Introduction

In 1997, the Aeronautical Charting Committee within the SAE International Aerospace Behavioral Engineering Technology Committee (SAE G-10) published Aerospace Recommended Practices (ARP) 5289, *Electronic Aeronautical Symbols* (SAE, 1997). This document contains industry-developed recommendations for symbols shown on electronic displays of charting information for aviation. The items covered in ARP 5289 are commonly used during operations under Instrument Flight Rules (IFR) (e.g., the missed approach track on instrument approach plates), although some of them (e.g., airspace boundaries) are also used under Visual Flight Rules (VFR).

In order to support the development of more standardized elements for electronic aeronautical displays, the SAE G-10 Aeronautical Charting Committee is updating ARP 5289. The updated document will be issued as ARP 5289A. In addition to addressing a variety of symbols, ARP 5289A will address lines and linear patterns, which are similar, but different, elements. The term *line* refers to an element typically used to denote a boundary. Lines vary from one another in terms of width (e.g., thick or thin) and/or style (e.g., dotted, dashed, bold). A *linear pattern* may also be used to denote a boundary, but it is represented by a set of repeated patterns or symbols (e.g., several x's along a row).

The SAE G-10 Aeronautical Charting Committee is taking a data-driven approach to determine which lines and linear patterns should have specific recommendations in ARP 5289A, and which can be left to the manufacturer's discretion. In particular, specific recommendations will be made for linear patterns that are considered to be very useful by pilots in an effort to standardize those linear patterns. The second use for the data is to identify whether there are some linear patterns that are currently well recognized and should be recommended for use as is. Well recognized patterns would be recommended both because they may aid pilots who are familiar with them and because they will reduce the potential conflicts (e.g., reuse of a well recognized pattern to represent a different type of information).

The current task for the John A. Volpe National Transportation Systems Center (Volpe Center), documented in this report, is to gather objective data upon which to base recommendations for lines and linear patterns. The goals of this study are to understand what lines and linear patterns are important to pilots, and to understand which, if any, linear patterns are currently well recognized. Tasks developed to address these goals are described in the Method section below.

Past research conducted by the Volpe Center in support of the electronic symbology recommendations is documented in various reports and papers (Yeh and Chandra, 2005; Yeh and Chandra, 2006; Chandra and Yeh, 2007; Chandra, Yeh, and Donovan, 2007). These studies focused on pilot recognition and identification of symbol shapes, such as navigation-aid symbols and other general symbols such as obstructions and markers. Further context and background for this series of studies is provided in these earlier reports. Funding and technical support for this research, including the current study, was provided by the Federal Aviation Administration (FAA).

Previous studies did not address lines on electronic charts and map displays in detail, although Chandra and Yeh (2007) did include a short exploration of line styles, in which pilot knowledge of line style conventions for paper charts and electronic map displays was assessed. The results showed that pilots are fairly knowledgeable about line conventions on paper charts, but that line conventions on electronic displays are not as well known or established. Lines and linear patterns currently in use by several manufacturers are documented in Yeh and Chandra (2008).

The SAE G-10 Aeronautical Charting Committee will consider the results of this research when developing ARP 5289A. The FAA or the International Civil Aviation Organization may choose to adopt this industry document by reference at a later date. The results of this research are also intended to be of use to industry manufacturers who develop and/or depict symbology. Note that the research effort is independent of the type of electronic display on which the lines and linear patterns are shown; the results apply regardless of the display's intended function. For example, the lines and linear patterns can be shown on electronic map displays, electronic chart displays, navigation displays, Electronic Flight Bags (EFBs), and multi-function displays.

2 Method

The study consisted of three tasks:

1) Line Sorting. Which lines and linear patterns are most useful?

2) Linear Pattern Recognition. Are there some linear patterns that are well recognized?

3) Subjective Comments. How important and useable are lines on paper and electronic displays overall?

The Line Sorting task is designed to address the SAE Aeronautical Charting Committee's goal of identifying which lines and linear patterns should be associated with specific recommendations. The Linear Pattern Recognition task addresses the SAE Aeronautical Charting Committee's other goal, to understand what current linear patterns are well recognized. In the last part of the study, pilots are asked to answer some general subjective questions on how they use line styles. These questions will help to understand the issues that pilots encounter in using the lines on charts in normal use.

The study was conducted in a paper format. Two versions were distributed, one in the Spring of 2007 (April through June), and the other in the Fall of 2007 (December). There were two minor differences between the Spring and Fall versions. First, the Spring version included a separate unrelated task that was not in the Fall version. Second, the Fall version had an updated background information form so that pilots could clearly specify that they had only a VFR rating.

The full Fall version of the survey is provided in Appendix A. The introductory sections that differed in the Spring version are provided in Appendix B. The tasks for each of these questions are described in more detail later in the report. Participants in the study and the general procedure for the study are described below.

2.1 Pilot Recruitment and Data-Collection Logistics

Pilots were recruited to participate from United States (US) domestic airlines, international airlines, the military, corporate operators, and private pilot organizations. A few of the pilots were Federal (US Government) employees from the FAA Flight Standards Service. International respondents to the survey were based in several countries (Australia, Canada, Denmark, England, Germany, Lebanon, Netherlands, New Zealand, and Mexico). Pilots were not compensated for their participation.

Distribution and collection of the data from international pilots was coordinated through the International Federation of Airline Pilots' Associations (IFALPA). For international participants, a point of contact within the local country received ten copies of the surveys, which he/she distributed and collected. When the local data collection was complete, the international point of contact returned all of the surveys back to the Volpe Center in one pre-paid shipment.

For the domestic airlines, the survey materials were distributed by a point of contact at the airline along with a preaddressed stamped envelope; pilots mailed the materials back directly to the Volpe Center. Similarly, military pilots received the materials through a point of contact at the Air Force Flight Standards Agency in Oklahoma City and mailed the materials back to the Volpe Center directly.

For the corporate operators and private pilots, an announcement about the study was posted on electronic newsletters, and pilots contacted the Volpe Center if they were interested in participating. The Volpe Center sent these pilots the paper materials along with a preaddressed stamped envelope for mailing back the materials.

2

Initially, all participants were required to be instrument-rated because the results were intended to generalize to pilots who routinely use charts for operations under IFR. However, input from non-instrument-rated private pilots was gathered later because many of those pilots also use electronic displays of charting information and their utilities for the different lines and linear patterns were expected to differ from that of instrument-rated pilots.

A total of 242 Spring surveys were distributed between April and June 2007, and 355 Fall surveys were distributed in December. Pilots were allowed three to four weeks to complete and return the surveys. Overall, 273 surveys were returned with signed informed consent forms, yielding a 46% response rate.

2.2   Pilot Background Information

Participants provided background information concerning their flight experience via the forms in Appendix A and Appendix B. The form gathered a variety of information including, ratings and certificates, flight experience, avionics experience, and chart experience. Participants indicated their type(s) of flight experience by checking items from a list of choices that included: Private-Instrument Flight Regulations (IFR), Private-Visual Flight Regulations (VFR), Private Business, Corporate, Air Transport, Military, International, and FAA/Regulatory.

Pilot demographic information is provided in Tables 1 through 9 for the overall sample and for the IFR and VFR Pilot groups separately. There were 130 pilots in the IFR Pilot group, which included pilots who reported either Instrument Ratings or Air Transport Pilot (ATP) ratings (which require knowledge of instrument procedures). All of the pilots who flew Air Transport operations, International operations, Corporate operations, and flight lengths over six hours held Instrument or ATP ratings and were therefore in the IFR Pilot group. The VFR Pilot group had 143 pilots, and included pilots who reported that they held only a Private Pilot (VFR Only) rating. Some of the VFR Pilots had instrument experience but were no longer current in instrument operations. For example, one VFR Pilot was a retired military pilot with 1200 hours of instrument time who was only *current* in Private VFR operations.

Table 1 shows the pilots' total flight hours and Table 2 shows the pilots' total instrument time. Table 3 shows the age distribution of the pilots, and Table 4 shows typical flight lengths. The VFR Pilots reported lower total flight hours. The VFR Pilot group also included a higher percentage of pilots 61 and older. Most pilots reported a typical flight length between one to three hours, with VFR Pilots flying more flights under one hour, and more IFR Pilots with flights longer than three hours.

Table 1. Total flight hours of experience.

Total Flight Hours	Overall	IFR Pilots	VFR Pilots
Minimum	62	170	62
Maximum	33000	33000	6000
Median	1500	9775	377.5

Table 2. Total instrument time.

Instrument Time	Overall	IFR Pilots	VFR Pilots
Minimum	0	10	0
Maximum	25000	25000	1200
Median	100	2630	5

3

Table 3. Age distribution.

Age	Overall	IFR Pilots	VFR Pilots
30 or under	5%	5%	4%
31 to 60	69%	80%	59%
61 or over	23%	12%	34%
Missing	3%	2%	3%

Table 4. Typical flight lengths.

Typical Flight Length	Overall	IFR Pilots	VFR Pilots
Under 1 hour	9%	4%	13%
1 to 3 hours	66%	51%	79%
3 to 6 hours	16%	29%	5%
Longer than 6 hours	7%	15%	0%
Missing	2%	2%	3%

Table 5 lists pilot ratings and certificates. Although only 118 participants reported that they held an instrument rating, 12 additional pilots reported that they held an Air Transport Pilot rating bringing the total size of the IFR Pilot group to 130. Table 6 shows the range of flight operations experience, and Table 7shows how several pilots actually had a mix of flight operations experiences.

Note that there were more pilots who held an Air Transport Pilot rating in the sample (108) than there were pilots who were actively flying Air Transport Operations (76). The ATP rating is not a requirement to fly Air Transport Operations, and having it does not necessarily imply that one is an airline pilot.

Similarly, there were more pilots in the sample who flew Private VFR Operations (177) than there were pilots who held only Private Pilot ratings (143). Some pilots with advance ratings were also flying Private VFR Operations.

Table 5. Pilot ratings and certificates.

Private Pilot Only (VFR)	143
Instrument Rating	118
Airline Transport Pilot Rating	108
Multi-Engine Rating	112
Commercial Certificate	91
Rotorcraft Rating	13

Table 6. Flight operations experience.

Private IFR Operations	23
Private VFR Operations	177
Private Business Operations	17
Corporate Operations	17
Air Transport Operations	76
Military Operations	14
International Operations	58
FAA/Regulatory Operations	11

Table 7. Pilots with mixed flight operations experience.

Flight Operations Experience	Private VFR	Private Business	Corporate	Air Transport	Military	International	FAA/ Regulatory
Private IFR	19	6	5	5	3	4	2
Private VFR		10	6	7	6	8	3
Private Business			4	4	0	4	1
Corporate				3	0	4	0
Air Transport					4	46	5
Military						4	2
International							7

Table 8 below provides a breakdown of chart experience. It was expected that IFR Pilots would be more likely to use Jeppesen charts, but the actual frequencies are not as one-sided as one might expect at first. Airline pilots often have Jeppesen experience, and in fact, 80% of the Air Transport pilots in this sample reported Jeppesen chart experience. However, the IFR Pilots in this sample also included Military pilots, FAA/Regulatory pilots, and Private IFR pilots, many of whom had NACO chart experience. Also, because of the large number of international air transport pilots in the study, many IFR Pilots reported experience with charts from manufacturers other than Jeppesen and NACO. The "Other" category of chart experience includes, for example, 13 users with Lido chart experience, seven with Mexican chart experience, and ten with SAS airline chart experience.

Table 8. Chart experience.

Chart Use	Overall	IFR Pilots	VFR Pilots
Jeppesen Only	23%	39%	8%
NACO Only	47%	18%	73%
Both Jeppesen and NACO	17%	18%	16%
Jeppesen and Other	6%	13%	0%
NACO and Other	1%	1%	1%
Other (only)	5%	11%	1%
Missing	0.4%	0%	0.7%

Table 9 below shows information about the pilots' avionics experience. As expected, the IFR Pilots are a more experienced group overall. However, over half of the VFR Pilot group also reported experience with map displays.

Table 9. Avionics experience.

	Overall	IFR Pilots	VFR Pilots
Glass Cockpit Experience	56%	85%	29%
Map Display Experience	60%	66%	55%
Traffic Display Experience	46%	83%	13%

2.3 Procedure

As mentioned earlier, the study was conducted via paper questionnaire. A cover letter provided explanatory information regarding the study and specifically asked participants to sign the Informed Consent form (Appendix A) so that their data could be included in the results.

The Spring version of the study consisted of two parts; the first part addressed line styles and the second was a separate unrelated task, which together lasted approximately 45 to 60 minutes. The Fall version of the study did not include the unrelated task, reducing the total experiment time by approximately

15 minutes. The total time for the study included time for short rest breaks, time to read the instructions and to complete the background questionnaire.

The three tasks in the study are described below.

2.3.1   Line Sorting

The goal of this task was to understand the utility that pilots have for various types of lines and linear patterns that are presented on chart and map displays. Using the instructions shown below in Figure 1, participants sorted the 65 items listed in Table 10 according to their usefulness. Some of items on this list are typically drawn as lines (e.g., Formation Radial or Bearing) and others are commonly drawn as linear patterns (e.g., Time Zone boundary).

The 65 items were printed on label sheets (one item on each label), in alphabetical order. Participants placed the labels for the two most useful categories onto separate sheets of paper, one that was titled "Items that I find to be very useful in general" and the other that was titled "Items that I recognize and use on occasion." Items that the participant did not commonly use, or did not recognize were to be left on the label sheets.

Appendix C contains definitions for some of the airspaces, regions, and zones listed in Table 10. For more information about the meaning and use of the individual items, consult the Federal Aviation Regulations/Aeronautical Information Manual (FAA, 2007) and/or the FAA Instrument Procedures Handbook (FAA, 2007).

(a) *Items that I find to be very useful in general.* These are items that you know well and refer to frequently. They should be easily identifiable. Place these items on the first sheet of paper.

(b) *Items that I recognize and use on occasion.* These are items that you use on occasion, but not as frequently as those you would place on the other sheet of paper. Place these items on the second sheet of paper.

(c) *Items that I do not commonly use, or I do not recognize.* These are items that you seldom use, or you are not sure of their meaning and need more information in order to understand their use. Leave these items on their original label sheet.

Figure 1. Instructions for Line Sorting task.

Table 10. List of lines and linear patterns to be sorted.

1. Air Defense Identification Zones (ADIZ)
2. Air Route Traffic Control Center (ARTCC)
3. Airport Radar Service Area (ARSA)
4. Alert Areas (A)
5. Alternate, Conditional or Uncontrolled Enroute Airway or ATS Route
6. Altimeter Setting Regions (QFE/QNH)
7. Balloon Launch Area
8. Bluff
9. Buffer Zone/Non-Free Flying Zone
10. Caution Areas (C)
11. City Pattern
12. Class A Airspace
13. Class B Airspace
14. Class C Airspace
15. Class D Airspace
16. Class E Airspace
17. Class F Airspace
18. Class G Airspace
19. CNS/ATM Equipment Reqmnt Areas (RNP, RVSM, MNPS, Mode C, etc.)
20. Contours
21. Control Area CTA/CTL
22. Control Zone/Air Traffic Zone (CTR/CTZ/ATZ)
23. Controlled Firing Area (CFA) (United States)
24. Country (State) Boundary
25. Danger Areas (D)
26. Enroute Airway or ATS Route
27. Enroute ATC Holding Pattern
28. Flight Information Region/Upper Flight Information Region (FIR/UIR)
29. Formation Radial or Bearing (Enroute & Terminal)
30. Helicopter Traffic Zone/Protected Zone (HTZ/HPZ)
31. International Date Line
32. Isogonic Lines

33. Lake or Pond
34. Military Control Zone/Military Air Traffic Zone (MCTR/MATZ)
35. Military Operations Area (MOA)
36. Missed Approach Procedure Holding Pattern
37. Missed Approach Procedure Track
38. National Security Area (NSA) (United States)
39. Oceanic Control Area (OCA)
40. Positive Control Area (PCA)
41. Prohibited Airspace Area (P)
42. Radar Vector Track
43. Railroad (single or multiple track)
44. Restricted Airspace Area (R)
45. River or Stream
46. Road (single or multi-lane)
47. Shoreline
48. Special Rules Area/Zone (SRA/SRZ)
49. Special VFR NA (Fixed Wing) Airspace
50. Speed Limit Area
51. Telephone or Power Lines
52. Temporary Flight Restriction Area (TFR)
53. Temporary Reserve/Segregated Areas (European equivalent of MOA)
54. Terminal ATC Holding Pattern
55. Terminal Control Area (TCA/TMA)
56. Terminal Procedure Course Reversal Holding Pattern
57. Terminal Procedure Flight Track
58. Terminal Radar Service Area (TRSA)
59. Terminal Transition or Feeder Route (Arrival, Departure, Approach)
60. Time Zone Boundary
61. Traffic Information Area/Zone (TIA/TIZ)
62. Training Areas (T)
63. Upper Control Area (UCA/UTA)
64. Visual Flight Track
65. Warning Area (W)

2.3.2 Linear Pattern Recognition

The goal of this task was to identify well-recognized linear patterns that could be adopted as recommended standards. The subject-matter-experts on the SAE Aeronautical Charting Committee considered the different linear patterns in use and proposed nine candidate patterns that might be well recognized, even without context, and one fake pattern. The purpose of the fake pattern was to identify a baseline for pilot recognition of the linear patterns; the fake pattern was expected to not be recognized because it is not actually used. Note also that two options were tested for the Air Defense Identification Zone (ADIZ). The source for ADIZ Option 1 was the ICAO linear pattern, and the source for ADIZ Option 2 was the Jeppesen and Lido linear patterns, which are similar to each other. No lines were tested in this part of the study, only linear patterns.

In this task, the participants saw the linear pattern, and were asked to identify it and indicate their confidence in the response. If they did not know what the linear pattern represented, they were instructed to place a "?" in the response field. The instructions for the task are shown in Figure 2, and a sample question is shown in Figure 3. (The instructions in Figure 2 use the term "line" pattern instead of "linear" pattern, but the intended meaning is the same.) The linear patterns that were tested are shown in Table 11.

The purpose of this task is to determine whether line patterns being proposed for use on electronic charts are well recognized. For each line pattern below, try to identify it and indicate the level of confidence in your response. Some of the line patterns are unusual, so you should not expect to be familiar with them all. Write "?" if you do not know what the line pattern represents.

Note that the patterns are drawn in black and white here, but they may be shown in color on an actual chart. Please disregard the lack of color.

Figure 2. Instructions for Linear Patterns Recognition task.

Line pattern (or ?): _____

1	2	3	4	5	6	7
Low			Medium			High
Confidence			Confidence			Confidence

Figure 3. Sample linear pattern question.

Table 11. Linear patterns tested.

Test Item	Linear Pattern	Source
Air Defense Identification Zone (ADIZ) Option 1		ICAO
Air Defense Identification Zone (ADIZ) Option 2		Jeppesen/Lido
Air Route Traffic Control Center (ARTCC)		NACO
Communications		Jeppesen
Flight Information Region (FIR)		Jeppesen
Fake Pattern	××××××××××××××	SAE
Controlled Airspace		ICAO
International Boundary		ICAO
Special Use Airspace Boundary		ICAO
Time Zone		Jeppesen

2.3.3 Subjective Questions

A few questions about the participants' use of lines on charts and map displays were posed in order to understand the overall importance of lines to their flight operations. These questions can be found in Appendix A.

In summary, subjects were asked to think of a typical flight, categorize its purpose (Air Transport, Private, Business/Corporate, or Military) and list some specific lines that are important for this typical flight. In addition, subjects responded to three questions on a numerical scale:

- How important would lines on charts/maps be to you during this typical flight?
  (1 = Low Importance, 4 = Medium Importance, 7 = High Importance)

- How often do you have difficulty interpreting lines on paper charts?
  (1 = Rarely, 4 = Sometimes, 7 = Frequently)

- How often do you have difficulty interpreting lines on electronic charts and map displays?
  (1 = Rarely, 4 = Sometimes, 7 = Frequently)

3 Analyses and Results

The 273 pilots in this study were separated into different groups for the purposes of the data analysis based on their responses to the background questionnaire. The groups were of four types, listed below.

1) Pilot Qualification, two exclusive options, either IFR or VFR.
   As noted earlier, the 130 IFR Pilots included all Air Transport, Corporate, and International operators. In addition, the IFR Pilot group included pilots who conducted Military operations, Private IFR operations, and even pilots who had experience with VFR operations, but were qualified for IFR operations. The VFR Pilot group included 143 pilots who were current only in VFR operations.

2) Flight Operations, eight non-exclusive options.
   As listed earlier (Table 6), there were eight types of flight operations. The options are non-

9

exclusive because each pilot could check off experience with one *or more* of these types of operations. In other words, pilots could indicate that they have more than one type of flight operation experience. Table 6 also shows the number of pilots in each of the flight operations groups.

3) Flight Length, four exclusive options.
Twenty-four pilots reported that their typical flight length was less than one hour, 179 reported a typical flight length between one to three hours, 45 reported a typical flight length between three to six hours, and 19 reported a typical flight length of six hours or longer. Six pilots did not report their typical flight length.

4) Chart Experience.
Because there were many pilots who reported experience with more than one type of chart, there are two different ways to think of this factor. One option is to regard pilot chart experience as *cumulative*, meaning that pilots could be knowledgeable about more than one chart type at a time. In this framework, a pilot could be counted as an experienced user of *both* charts with which they were familiar. Counting this way, of the 273 pilots in the sample, 123 had Jeppesen chart experience, 177 had NACO chart experience, and 13 had Lido chart experience.

A second way to think of chart experience is to try to tease out as much information about the effect of chart experience as possible by excluding all pilots who reported experience with multiple chart types from the sample, and only comparing those who reported exclusive use of one chart type (e.g., Jeppesen only) against those who were exclusive users of another chart type (e.g., NACO). With this method, many of the participants had to be dropped from the data set, leaving just 63 exclusive Jeppesen chart users and 129 exclusive NACO chart users.

The analyses for the two tasks, Line Sorting and Linear Pattern Recognition were both conducted with these categories in mind. However, it must be recognized that these categories are not independent. The correlations between the pilot groups and flight experience are explored in the next section, prior to the analysis of the results for each of the specific tasks.

3.1 Correlations Between Pilot Groups

Jeppesen chart users tended to have significantly more flight hours of experience ($r = 0.53$, $p < 0.001$). They also tended to be instrument rated; 72% of pilots with Jeppesen experience were in the IFR Pilot group ($r = 0.46$, $p < 0.001$). And, Jeppesen chart users tended to fly longer flights on average ($r = 0.34$, $p < 0.001$). Most NACO users (73%) were VFR Pilots ($r = 0.56$, $p < 0.001$), had lower total flight hours ($r = 0.63$, $p < 0.001$), and flew shorter flights on average ($r = 0.45$, $p < 0.001$).

The correlations reported above are part or a larger correlation matrix, which is provided in full in Table 12 below. Correlation coefficients are reported in all cases where they were statistically significant. Cells for which the correlation coefficient was not statistically significant contain the entry "NS." Cells with positive correlations are shaded in bright yellow for values greater than 0.5 and in dull yellow for smaller values. Large negative correlations (greater than 0.5) are shaded in bright blue and smaller values are shaded in dull green. All of the correlation coefficients were significant at the $p < 0.01$ level or better except for those marked with a single asterisk, which were significant at the $p < 0.05$ level. The number of pilots in each group is shown in the title of each column as a reminder of the sample size.

Note that the column labeled "VFR/IFR Pilots" in Table 12 actually represents the relations to both IFR and VFR Pilots because the pilot could only be one or the other. Because of the way the variable was coded in the data set ("true" for VFR Pilots, and "false" for IFR pilots), *positive* correlations in the VFR Pilots column indicate a positive relationship with the VFR Pilot group, and negative correlations in the VFR Pilot column represent a *positive* relationship with the IFR Pilot group.

The columns and rows in Table 12, and the shading of the cells, are arranged to show that there were two distinct ends of the pilot spectrum. The spectrum that emerges from the data in Table 12makes intuitive sense from a practical perspective. On one side are the pilots with air transport and international experience, longer flight lengths, more overall flight hours, and Jeppesen chart experience. On the other side of the pilot spectrum are pilots who fly VFR operations, use NACO charts, and fly shorter flights. In between these two ends are the pilots who fly Private IFR, Private Business, and Corporate operations. Military pilots tend to use NACO charts, but are otherwise not significantly like either of the two ends of the pilot spectrum. Similarly, the FAA/Regulatory pilots are difficult to categorize, though they are similar to the Military pilots and also to the International pilots. Note that the sample sizes were smallest for the FAA/Regulatory and Military pilots groups as well, so there may not have been enough data for strong statistically significant findings.

The significant implication of Table 12 is that it is difficult to identify a *single* factor as being *the* most important explanation for a particular response to the Line Sorting task or to the Linear Patterns Recognition task. For example, a particular element that achieved a low recognition by the Air Transport pilot group would also likely have received a low recognition for the highly correlated group of Jeppesen users, and it will be difficult to identify whether the item was poorly recognized *because* of the experience with Air Transport *operations* or because of the familiarity with Jeppesen *charts*. In addition, the underlying factors could vary for every one of the items that were rated, either in the Line Sorting task, or in the Linear Pattern Recognition task, making the detailed analysis even more complex.

Table 12. Correlations among the pilot characteristics and experience.

	VFR/IFR Pilots (143 VFR/130 IFR)	Private VFR (177)	NACO Experience (177)	Private Business (17)	Corporate (17)	Military (14)	FAA/Regulatory (11)	Private IFR (23)	Lido Experience (13)	Jeppesen Experience (123)	Flight Length	International (58)	Air Transport (76)	Flight Hours
VFR/IFR Pilots	1	0.74	0.56	-0.18	-0.27	-0.21	-0.22	-0.32	-0.24	-0.46	-0.46	-0.55	-0.65	-0.73
Private VFR	0.74	1	0.60	NS	-0.16	NS	-0.16	NS	-0.23	-0.44	-0.52	-0.56	-0.72	-0.68
NACO Experience	0.56	0.60	1	NS	NS	0.14*	NS	NS	-0.20	-0.55	-0.45	-0.54	-0.67	-0.63
Private Business	-0.18	NS	NS	1	0.19	NS	NS	0.25	NS	NS	NS	NS	NS	NS
Corporate	-0.27	-0.16	NS	0.19	1	NS	NS	0.20	NS	0.25	NS	NS	NS	0.20
Military	-0.21	NS	0.14*	NS	NS	1	0.12*	NS	NS	NS	NS	NS	NS	NS
FAA/Regulatory	-0.22	-0.16	NS	NS	NS	0.12*	1	NS	0.13*	0.15*	NS	0.21	NS	NS
Private IFR	-0.32	NS	NS	0.25	0.20	NS	NS	1	NS	NS	NS	NS	NS	NS
Lido Experience	-0.24	-0.23	-0.20	NS	NS	NS	0.13*	NS	1	NS	0.20	0.18	0.32	0.20
Jeppesen Experience	-0.46	-0.44	-0.55	NS	0.25	NS	0.15*	NS	NS	1	0.34	0.35	0.43	0.53
Flight Length	-0.46	-0.52	-0.45	NS	NS	NS	NS	NS	0.20	0.34	1	0.59	0.57	0.57
International	-0.55	-0.56	-0.54	NS	NS	NS	0.21	NS	0.18	0.35	0.59	1	0.60	0.64
Air Transport	-0.65	-0.72	-0.67	NS	NS	NS	NS	NS	0.32	0.43	0.57	0.60	1	0.71
Flight Hours	-0.73	-0.68	-0.63	NS	0.20	NS	NS	NS	0.20	0.53	0.57	0.64	0.71	1

Note. NS denotes non-significant values. Values marked with an asterisk are significant at $p < 0.05$; all others are significant at $p < 0.01$. Strong positive correlations appear in the top left and bottom right. Strong negative correlations appear in the bottom left and top right.

3.2 Line Sorting

Each pilot sorted each of the 65 lines and linear patterns into one of three categories: Very Useful, Recognize/Use on Occasion, and Do Not Use/Do Not Recognize. To understand how useful the items were overall, the responses were tallied within various pilot groups. A statistical test (Chi-square) was then performed on the data to determine which airspaces and boundaries received a statistically significant number of responses in each response category for each pilot group. In this case, the test determined whether the number of responses in the category was statistically different from chance, which would have produced evenly distributed responses, i.e., 1/3 in each of the three response categories. The statistical test is more sensitive when there are more data, so results for the smaller sample size groups are less definitive.

Four types of pilot groups were described at the beginning of this section: Pilot Qualification, Flight Operations, Flight Length, and Chart Experience. For the analysis of the line sorting responses, the Chart Experience groups were not considered. This was because pilots sorted the lines based only on their *names* and the value of the information those names represented. There were no sample images provided for the Line Sorting task, so it was not expected that the actual linear patterns used on different charts would influence how the items were sorted. Because chart experience is correlated with other variables (e.g., flight length, and flight operations), a statistical analysis of the effect of chart experience will show significant results in the same direction as the correlations would indicate, but this does not produce any new insights into the data.

Three tables below provide an overview of the items that were found to be Very Useful with the statistical test. Table 13 lists the items that were considered to be Very Useful broken down by IFR Pilots and VFR Pilots. Table 14 lists the items that were considered to be Very Useful broken down by Flight Operation. Table 15 lists the items that were considered to be Very Useful broken down by Flight Length.

Detailed results for each item, including which items were in the Do Not Use/Do Not Recognize category from the Line Sorting task are provided in Appendix D for each of the fourteen pilot groups considered (IFR and VFR Pilots, eight types of Flight Operations, and four Flight Lengths). Appendix D may be useful to manufacturers who seek more detailed information when determining what items should be provided on a given display. In addition to showing statistically significant results, Appendix D provides information on trends in the results.

Note that in Table 14, Class B Airspace is not marked as Very Useful for Air Transport and International operations, whereas it is useful to all other pilot groups. In the same table, Terminal Control Area (TCA/TMA) is only marked as Very Useful by Air Transport and International pilots, and no other pilot groups. This result is bit confusing because Class B Airspace is just the new name for the old term Terminal Control Area (TCA/TMA), and both items were therefore expected to receive similar ratings. The two terms were only included in the study due to an oversight.

Results for these two items are compared directly in Table 16. For groups that rated the item significantly Very Useful the cell contains $\oplus\oplus\oplus$. For groups that rated the item as significantly Do Not Use/Do Not Recognize the cell contains a $\Downarrow$ symbol. Blank cells indicate that there was no statistically significant direction for the responses.

The results shown in Table 16 indicate that pilots who fly Air Transport and International operations, particularly those who fly long flights, appear to be more familiar with the old term (TCA/TMA) than the new term (Class B Airspace). VFR Pilots, who fly shorter flight lengths, are more familiar with the new term. These differences in familiarity with the terms provide an explanation for the inconsistency seen in.

Table 13. Items considered Very Useful by IFR Pilots and VFR Pilots (26).

Item	IFR Pilots	VFR Pilots
Air Defense Identification Zones (ADIZ)	x	x
Class B Airspace	x	x
Class C Airspace	x	x
Class D Airspace	x	x
Prohibited Airspace Area (P)	x	x
Restricted Airspace Area (R)	x	x
Enroute ATC Holding Pattern	x	
Missed Approach Procedure Holding Pattern	x	
Missed Approach Procedure Track	x	
Terminal ATC Holding Pattern	x	
Terminal Procedure Flight Track	x	
Terminal Transition or Feeder Route (Arrival, Departure, Approach)	x	
Enroute Airway or ATS Route	x	
Terminal Control Area (TCA/TMA)	x	
Warning Area (W)	x	
Telephone or Power Lines		x
City Pattern		x
Class E Airspace		x
Contours		x
Lake or Pond		x
Military Operations Area (MOA)		x
Railroad (single or multiple track)		x
River or Stream		x
Road (single or multi-lane)		x
Shoreline		x
Temporary Flight Restriction Area (TFR)		x

Table 14. Items considered Very Useful by type of flight operation (30).

Item	Private IFR	Private VFR	Private Business	Corporate	Air Transport	Military	International	FAA/Regulatory
Air Defense Identification Zones (ADIZ)		x	x					x
City Pattern		x						
Class B Airspace	x	x	x	x		x		x
Class C Airspace	x	x	x	x	x	x	x	x
Class D Airspace	x	x	x	x		x		
Class E Airspace		x						
CNS/ATM Equipment Requirement Areas (RNP, RVSM, MNPS, Mode C, etc.)					x		x	
Contours		x						
Control Zone/Air Traffic Zone (CTR/CTZ/ATZ)					x		x	
Danger Areas (D)					x		x	
Enroute Airway or ATS Route	x				x	x	x	x
Enroute ATC Holding Pattern					x			
Flight Information Region/Upper Flight Information Region (FIR/UIR)					x		x	
Lake or Pond		x		x				
Military Operations Area (MOA)	x	x	x	x		x		
Missed Approach Procedure Holding Pattern	x			x	x	x	x	x
Missed Approach Procedure Track	x				x	x	x	x
Prohibited Airspace Area (P)	x	x	x	x	x	x	x	
Railroad (single or multiple track)		x						
Restricted Airspace Area (R)	x	x	x	x	x	x	x	
River or Stream		x		x				
Road (single or multi-lane)		x						
Shoreline		x						
Telephone or Power Lines		x						
Temporary Flight Restriction Area (TFR)	x	x	x	x				
Terminal ATC Holding Pattern					x		x	x
Terminal Control Area (TCA/TMA)					x		x	
Terminal Procedure Flight Track					x	x	x	
Terminal Transition or Feeder Route (Arrival, Departure, Approach)					x	x	x	x
Warning Area (W)		x				x	x	

14

Table 15. Items considered Very Useful by typical flight length (29).

Item	Less than 1 Hr	1 to 3 Hrs	3 to 6 Hrs	Longer than 6 Hrs
Air Defense Identification Zones (ADIZ)		x	x	
City Pattern		x		
Class B Airspace	x	x	x	
Class C Airspace	x	x	x	x
Class D Airspace	x	x		
Class E Airspace		x		
CNS/ATM Equipment Requirement Areas (RNP, RVSM, MNPS, Mode C, etc.)				x
Contours		x		
Control Area (CTA/CTL)				x
Enroute Airway or ATS Route		x	x	x
Enroute ATC Holding Pattern				x
Flight Information Region/Upper Flight Information Region (FIR/UIR)				x
Lake or Pond	x	x		
Military Operations Area (MOA)	x	x		
Missed Approach Procedure Holding Pattern			x	x
Missed Approach Procedure Track			x	x
Oceanic Control Area (OCA)				x
Prohibited Airspace Area (P)	x	x	x	x
Railroad (single or multiple track)	x	x		
Restricted Airspace Area (R)	x	x	x	
River or Stream	x	x		
Road (single or multi-lane)	x	x		
Shoreline		x		
Telephone or Power Lines		x		
Temporary Flight Restriction Area (TFR)	x	x		
Terminal Control Area (TCA/TMA)				x
Terminal Transition or Feeder Route (Arrival, Departure, Approach)				x
Upper Control Area (UCA/UTA)				x
Warning Area (W)		x	x	

Table 16. Comparison of results for two items, Class B Airspace and Terminal Control Area (TCA/TMA).

Pilot Group	Class B Airspace	Terminal Control Area (TCA/TMA)
IFR Pilots	⊕⊕⊕	⊕⊕⊕
VFR Pilots	⊕⊕⊕	⇓
Private IFR	⊕⊕⊕	
Private VFR	⊕⊕⊕	⇓
Private Business	⊕⊕⊕	
Corporate	⊕⊕⊕	
Air Transport		⊕⊕⊕
Military	⊕⊕⊕	
International		⊕⊕⊕
FAA/Regulatory	⊕⊕⊕	
Less than 1 Hr	⊕⊕⊕	
1-3 Hr	⊕⊕⊕	⇓
3-6 Hr	⊕⊕⊕	
6+ Hr		⊕⊕⊕

Table 17 and Table 18 show the utility of each tested item across pilot groups. These tables summarize the more complex view of results provided in Appendix C (which is similar to the data shown in Table 16 above) by recording, for each item, how many of the 14 pilot groups considered it to be Very Useful, had mixed results, or considered it to be not used/recognized.

Table 17 shows the 33 items for which at least one pilot group considered the item to be Very Useful. Items at the top of Table 17 are generally useful to most of the pilots in the study. Items towards the bottom of Table 17 are useful to some, but not all groups. In some cases an item was Very Useful to one group, and not recognized/used by another. For example, items such as Missed Approach Procedure Track and Missed Approach Procedure Holding Pattern are Very Useful to some groups (IFR Pilots, Air Transport, etc.) and not recognized or used by others (VFR Pilots, Private VFR operators, etc.). Another item in this category is the Temporary Flight Restriction (TFR), which is not recognized/used by the Air Transport and International pilots, but is Very Useful to most other pilot groups. Three related items (Control Area, Oceanic Control Area, and Upper Control Area) are only useful to one group of pilots, those who fly the longest (over 6 hour) flights.

Table 18 lists 32 items for which not one pilot group considered the item to be Very Useful. Items at the top of Table 18 have mixed results, indicating that they may have been somewhat useful, but were not Very Useful. Items towards the bottom of Table 18 are generally not useful to or recognized by any group of pilots.

Table 17. Summary of responses from the 14 pilot groups for the 33 items considered Very Useful by at least one pilot group.

Item	Very Useful	Mixed Responses	Do Not Use/ Do Not Recognize
Class C Airspace	14	0	0
Prohibited Airspace Area (P)	13	1	0
Restricted Airspace Area (R)	12	2	0
Class B Airspace	11	3	0
Class D Airspace	9	5	0
Enroute Airway or ATS Route	9	5	0
Missed Approach Procedure Holding Pattern	9	1	4
Military Operations Area (MOA)	8	6	0
Missed Approach Procedure Track	8	2	4
Air Defense Identification Zones (ADIZ)	7	7	0
Temporary Flight Restriction Area (TFR)	7	5	2
Terminal Transition or Feeder Route (Arrival, Departure, Approach)	6	4	4
Warning Area (W)	6	8	0
Lake or Pond	5	9	0
River or Stream	5	7	2
Railroad (single or multiple track)	4	5	5
Road (single or multi-lane)	4	7	3
Terminal ATC Holding Pattern	4	6	4
Terminal Control Area (TCA/TMA)	4	7	3
Terminal Procedure Flight Track	4	6	4
City Pattern	3	8	3
Class E Airspace	3	11	0
CNS/ATM Equipment Requirement Areas (RNP, RVSM, MNPS, Mode C, etc.)	3	6	5
Contours	3	11	0
Enroute ATC Holding Pattern	3	7	4
Flight Information Region/Upper Flight Information Region (FIR/UIR)	3	5	6
Shoreline	3	11	0
Telephone or Power Lines	3	6	5
Control Zone/Air Traffic Zone (CTR/CTZ/ATZ)	2	9	3
Danger Areas (D)	2	6	6
Control Area (CTA/CTL)	1	5	8
Oceanic Control Area (OCA)	1	6	7
Upper Control Area (UCA/UTA)	1	4	9

17

Table 18. Summary of responses from the 14 pilot groups for the 32 items not considered to be Very Useful by any one of the pilot groups.

Item	Very Useful	Mixed Responses	Do Not Use/ Do Not Recognize
Alert Areas (A)	0	14	0
Country (State) Boundary	0	14	0
Terminal Radar Service Area (TRSA)	0	14	0
Air Route Traffic Control Center (ARTCC)	0	12	2
Class A Airspace	0	11	3
Isogonic Lines	0	11	3
Airport Radar Service Area (ARSA)	0	10	4
Terminal Procedure Course Reversal Holding Pattern	0	10	4
Time Zone Boundary	0	10	4
Caution Areas (C)	0	9	5
Altimeter Setting Regions (QFE/QNH)	0	8	6
Visual Flight Track	0	8	6
Class G Airspace	0	7	7
Speed Limit Area	0	6	8
International Date Line	0	5	9
Balloon Launch Area	0	4	10
Class F Airspace	0	4	10
Formation Radial or Bearing (Enroute & Terminal)	0	4	10
Military Control Zone/Military Air Traffic Zone (MCTR/MATZ)	0	4	10
National Security Area (NSA) (United States)	0	4	10
Positive Control Area (PCA)	0	4	10
Radar Vector Track	0	4	10
Training Areas (T)	0	4	10
Alternate, Conditional or Uncontrolled Enroute Airway or ATS Route	0	3	11
Special VFR NA (Fixed Wing) Airspace	0	3	11
Bluff	0	2	12
Controlled Firing Area (CFA) (United States)	0	2	12
Special Rules Area/Zone (SRA/SRZ)	0	2	12
Traffic Information Area/Zone (TIA/TIZ)	0	2	12
Buffer Zone/Non-Free Flying Zone	0	1	13
Helicopter Traffic Zone/Protected Zone (HTZ/HPZ)	0	1	13
Temporary Reserve/Segregated Areas (European equivalent of MOA)	0	1	13

3.3 Linear Pattern Recognition

Pilots were asked to identify a linear pattern by writing in its name and/or a description. Nine linear patterns were tested along with one fake pattern, which is not in use today. The symbols were presented as line segments without the context normally seen in a charting display. Clues such as the shape of the boundary, its length or size relative to other features, and its position relative to other features can all help a pilot identify its meaning, but none of these clues were available in this experimental task.

Responses varied because of the free-response nature of the task; in other words, pilots sometimes used different words to express similar concepts. In order to understand the results, the responses were coded into categories. The categories were constructed with the aid of the SAE G-10 Aeronautical Charting Committee. The Committee reviewed a partial set of data (the first 50 responses) to help the Volpe Center team to determine which responses were correct and which were not if there was any question about the response. (For example, the Committee determined that "Air Traffic Control *Sector* Boundary" was an incorrect response to the linear pattern that showed an Air Traffic Control *Center* Boundary," because a *Sector* is just one part of the *Center*.) Final results of the analysis indicate how accurately the symbols were recognized. A similar process for handling responses is described in Chandra and Yeh (2007) in more detail.

Preliminary testing of the linear patterns indicated that the identification task would be difficult without context, and the final data confirmed this expectation. Many of the responses were either missing or "Can't Tell," as detailed below in Table 19 for each item. The Can't Tell response confirms that the pilot did not know what the linear pattern represented, but the missing response does not; the pilot may have left the item blank for other reasons. Therefore, when determining overall accuracy, "Can't Tell" responses were considered incorrect, and missing responses were excluded from the analysis. Notice that the fake pattern was actually the most difficult pattern for the participants to identify, as expected.

Table 19. Overall difficulty of the linear pattern recognition task.

Test Item	% Can't Tell Responses	% Missing Responses	Sum of Can't Tell and Missing Responses
Fake Pattern	70%	13%	83%
ADIZ Option 2 (Jeppesen/Lido)	68%	11%	79%
Communications	60%	10%	70%
Flight Information Region (FIR)	44%	26%	70%
Air Route Traffic Control Center (ARTCC)	58%	11%	69%
Time Zone	37%	26%	63%
ADIZ Option 1 (ICAO)	36%	22%	58%
International Boundary	32%	25%	57%
Controlled Airspace	24%	26%	50%
Special Use Airspace Boundary	22%	11%	33%

The responses that were provided for the linear pattern task varied less than the responses obtained for the symbols tested in Chandra and Yeh (2007), so the assessment of which responses were correct was more straightforward. For most items, the correct answer, missing, and Can't Tell responses accounted for over 90% of the responses, so there were relatively few incorrect responses. In several cases the incorrect answers were too generic for classification (e.g., "boundary"). In other cases, the incorrect answers showed no particular pattern.

Overall accuracy and confidence in the correct response for each of the test patterns is shown in Table 20 below. The Special Use Airspace (SUA) boundary obtained the highest overall accuracy rate across all pilots in the sample (51%). Note that a wide range of responses was acceptable for this item. Any specific example of an SUA boundary, (e.g., Restricted Airspace, Military Operations Area) was considered to be correct. Responses that mentioned other types of restrictions (e.g., ADIZ, speed limit area) were considered incorrect (17%).

The International boundary also obtained a relatively high level of recognition (43%). Here too, a wide variety of responses was considered acceptable. In particular, responses that mentioned either "State" boundaries or country/international boundaries were acceptable because ICAO uses the term "State" to represent different international entities. However, in the United States, "State" generally refers to different areas within the country. As a result, some pilots who used the term "state" may or may not have known that the boundary represents an international demarcation. One response that was occasionally confused with the International boundary was the Magnetic Variation line (also known as an Isogonic line), which was mentioned in 5% of the responses.

A few other relatively minor confusions were noted with some of the linear patterns. For the Controlled Airspace pattern, the most common incorrect answer was Mode C Veil, which was mentioned in 7% of the responses. The Mode C Veil refers to the requirement in the United States to have a Mode C transponder for operations in the area. It is often shown in the vicinity of Class B and Class C airspace. For the ICAO ADIZ linear pattern a few pilots (less than 5%) mentioned Reduced Vertical Separation Minima (RVSM). A few pilots (less than 5%) mentioned ARTCC boundaries in response to the Communications boundary pattern. Some pilots (3%) mentioned Airspace in response to the ARTCC linear pattern. A few pilots (3%) mentioned ARTCC as a response to the Flight Information Region (FIR) boundary.

Table 20. Overall accuracy of and confidence in linear pattern recognition.

Test Item	Overall Accuracy	Average Confidence in Correct Response	Number of Responses
SUA Boundary	51%	5.21	243
Controlled Airspace	43%	5.37	203
International Boundary	43%	5.71	206
ADIZ Option 1 (ICAO)	35%	4.88	212
Time Zone	30%	5.53	202
Flight Information Region (FIR)	28%	5.81	201
ARTCC	18%	5.36	242
Communications	16%	6.1	245
ADIZ Option 2 (Jeppesen/Lido)	16%	5.05	243

3.3.1   Recognition Accuracy as a Function of Pilot Group

For a more detailed look at the accuracy results, the accuracies were computed for each of 17 pilot groups. These included the same 14 pilot groups used in the Line Sorting task analysis, and also include three categories of chart user experience (Jeppesen Experience, NACO Experience, and Lido Experience). For this analysis, chart experience was considered to be *cumulative*, meaning that pilots could be knowledgeable about more than one chart type at a time, as discussed in Section 3 above.

Each of the tables below (Table 21 through Table 29) shows the accuracies for each of the pilot groups for each of the tested symbols. Each table is sorted in order of decreasing accuracy, with the overall accuracy across all pilot groups also indicated.

Table 21. Accuracy by pilot group for recognition of the Special Use Airspace boundary linear pattern.

Special Use Airspace Boundary	
Pilot Group	**Accuracy**
Military	71.4%
Flight Length <1 Hr	70.0%
Private IFR	65.2%
Private Business	62.5%
NACO Experience	54.8%
IFR Pilots	53.8%
Corporate	53.3%
Jeppesen Experience	53.2%
Flight Length 6+ Hr	50.0%
Private VFR	49.4%
Flight Length 3-6 Hr	48.7%
Flight Length 1-3 Hr	48.4%
Air Transport	47.8%
VFR Pilots	47.6%
International	46.2%
FAA/Regulatory	45.5%
Lido Experience	30.8%
Overall Average	**50.6%**

Table 22. Accuracy by pilot group for recognition of the Flight Information Region linear pattern.

Flight Information Region	
Pilot Group	**Accuracy**
Flight Length 6+ Hr	77.8%
International	70.6%
Air Transport	60.6%
FAA/Regulatory	50.0%
Flight Length 3-6 Hr	50.0%
IFR Pilots	46.7%
Jeppesen Experience	45.3%
Military	38.5%
Lido Experience	36.4%
Corporate	28.6%
Private Business	23.1%
Flight Length 1-3 Hr	16.8%
Private IFR	16.7%
NACO Experience	12.7%
Private VFR	10.0%
Flight Length <1 Hr	7.7%
VFR Pilots	7.3%
Overall Average	**27.9%**

Table 23. Accuracy by pilot group for recognition of the Communications boundary linear pattern.

Communications Boundary	
Pilot Group	Accuracy
FAA/Regulatory	55.6%
Lido Experience	53.8%
Flight Length 3-6 Hr	48.8%
International	48.1%
Air Transport	44.9%
Flight Length 6+ Hr	44.4%
IFR Pilots	34.5%
Jeppesen Experience	33.6%
Corporate	33.3%
Private Business	31.3%
Military	21.4%
Private IFR	17.4%
Flight Length 1-3 Hr	7.5%
NACO Experience	6.3%
Private VFR	3.2%
Flight Length <1 Hr	0.0%
VFR Pilots	0.0%
Overall Average	**16.3%**

Table 24. Accuracy by pilot group for recognition of the ICAO ADIZ linear pattern.

ADIZ Option 1 (ICAO)	
Pilot Group	Accuracy
Flight Length <1 Hr	62.5%
FAA/Regulatory	50.0%
VFR Pilots	49.1%
NACO Experience	48.1%
Private IFR	47.1%
Private VFR	45.7%
Flight Length 1-3 Hr	40.7%
Corporate	37.5%
Military	30.8%
Jeppesen Experience	28.6%
Private Business	25.0%
IFR Pilots	21.7%
Lido Experience	20.0%
Flight Length 3-6 Hr	17.1%
Flight Length 6+ Hr	11.1%
International	10.2%
Air Transport	9.2%
Overall Average	**35.4%**

Table 25. Accuracy by pilot group for recognition of the Controlled Airspace linear pattern.

Controlled Airspace	
Pilot Group	Accuracy
Private Business	66.7%
Corporate	57.1%
Private IFR	50.0%
VFR Pilots	49.0%
Private VFR	46.8%
NACO Experience	46.1%
Flight Length 1-3 Hr	44.8%
Jeppesen Experience	43.6%
FAA/Regulatory	42.9%
Flight Length <1 Hr	41.2%
Flight Length 6+ Hr	38.9%
Flight Length 3-6 Hr	38.7%
IFR Pilots	36.9%
International	35.6%
Air Transport	34.4%
Military	16.7%
Lido Experience	0.0%
Overall Average	**42.9%**

Table 26. Accuracy by pilot group for recognition of the Time Zone linear pattern.

Time Zone	
Pilot Group	Accuracy
Corporate	64.3%
Private Business	63.6%
FAA/Regulatory	57.1%
Lido Experience	55.6%
Air Transport	53.0%
Flight Length 3-6 Hr	51.5%
International	48.9%
Jeppesen Experience	46.8%
IFR Pilots	45.1%
Flight Length 6+ Hr	44.4%
Private IFR	43.8%
Flight Length 1-3 Hr	24.2%
NACO Experience	19.7%
Private VFR	16.4%
Military	15.4%
VFR Pilots	14.0%
Flight Length <1 Hr	12.5%
Overall Average	**29.6%**

Table 27. Accuracy by pilot group for recognition of the International boundary linear pattern.

International Boundary	
Pilot Group	**Accuracy**
FAA/Regulatory	57.1%
VFR Pilots	50.5%
NACO Experience	48.0%
Private VFR	48.0%
Flight Length 1-3 Hr	46.4%
Corporate	42.9%
Flight Length <1 Hr	42.9%
Jeppesen Experience	42.1%
Flight Length 3-6 Hr	39.4%
Private IFR	35.3%
IFR Pilots	35.0%
Air Transport	34.3%
International	31.3%
Private Business	27.3%
Military	25.0%
Flight Length 6+ Hr	22.2%
Lido Experience	.0%
Overall Average	**42.7%**

Table 28. Accuracy by pilot group for recognition of the ARTCC linear pattern.

ARTCC	
Pilot Group	**Accuracy**
Private IFR	54.5%
FAA/Regulatory	33.3%
Military	30.8%
Corporate	26.7%
Private Business	26.7%
NACO Experience	24.8%
IFR Pilots	20.4%
Flight Length 1-3 Hr	20.2%
Flight Length <1 Hr	20.0%
Private VFR	19.6%
Jeppesen Experience	16.7%
VFR Pilots	16.3%
Flight Length 3-6 Hr	15.8%
Lido Experience	15.4%
Air Transport	9.1%
Flight Length 6+ Hr	6.3%
International	4.1%
Overall Average	**18.2%**

Table 29. Accuracy by pilot group for recognition of the Jeppesen/Lido ADIZ linear pattern.

ADIZ Option 2 (Jeppesen/Lido)	
Pilot Group	**Accuracy**
Flight Length 3-6 Hr	46.3%
Flight Length 6+ Hr	44.4%
International	43.4%
Air Transport	38.6%
Lido Experience	30.8%
IFR Pilots	28.2%
Jeppesen Experience	27.9%
FAA/Regulatory	22.2%
Corporate	18.8%
Private IFR	18.2%
Private Business	17.6%
Military	8.3%
Flight Length 1-3 Hr	6.3%
NACO Experience	5.8%
Private VFR	5.8%
VFR Pilots	4.0%
Flight Length <1 Hr	0.0%
Overall Average	**15.6%**

3.3.2   Statistical Analyses of Recognition Accuracy

Because several pilot groups overlap with each other (i.e., there are subjects who are in more than one of the groups, in particular for the different flight operations experience types), it is not possible to do a direct statistical comparison between each of the group accuracies reported in Table 21 through Table 29. However, direct comparisons are possible for the groups that were distinct from one other. Specifically, Analyses of Variance (ANOVAs) were preformed to identify whether there were differences between the IFR and VFR Pilot groups, differences between the pilots who reported different typical flight lengths, and differences between the exclusive chart users of Jeppesen or NACO charts. No tests were conducted on the different flight operations categories because they were not exclusive, and because many pilots indicated more than one type of flight operations experience.

Note that the correlations matrix (Table 12) is relevant to the interpretation of ANOVAs. For example, because IFR Pilots tended to be users of Jeppesen charts, any affects found for IFR Pilots could also be due, at least in part, to chart experience, not just the pilot knowledge and use of the lines for IFR operations. Similarly, because IFR pilots tended to fly longer flight lengths, the results of the flight length ANOVA also could reflect the pilot qualifications and knowledge, and not just the actual flight length.

Results of the ANOVAs on the accuracy of recognized the nine tested linear patterns are summarized in Table 30. For cases where no statistically significant effect was found, the cell in the table contains "NS," for "not significant." Where a statistically significant effect was found, the means for the different groups and the value of the F-statistic are provided in the table. The F-statistic includes a probability level (p) that indicates the strength of the finding; lower p values indicate higher levels of statistical significance.

For two items, the SUA boundary and Controlled Airspace, none of the three ANOVAs found any significant effect. For the International boundary, there was no significance of the flight length or chart experience, but there was a significant difference between IFR and VFR Pilots. However, as noted above, many of the VFR Pilots who used the term "state" may have been referring to a state within the United States, so the interpretation of accuracy for this item is somewhat unclear.

25

Table 30. Summary of results from ANOVAs on accuracy of recognizing the tested linear patterns.

Test Item	Exclusive Jeppesen vs. Exclusive NACO Users	IFR vs. VFR Pilots	Flight Length
SUA Boundary	NS	NS	NS
Controlled Airspace	NS	NS	NS
International Boundary	NS	50% for VFR Pilots 35% for IFR Pilots $[F_{(1, 204)} = 5.16, p < 0.05]$	NS
ADIZ Option 1 (ICAO)	46% for NACO Only 14% for Jeppesen Only $[F_{(1, 204)} = 5.16, p < 0.05]$	49% for VFR Pilots 22% for IFR Pilots $[F_{(1, 210)} = 18.7, p < 0.001]$	63% for < 1 Hr Flight 41% for 1 to 3 Hr Flight 17% for 3 to 6 Hr Flight 11% for 6+ Hr Flight $[F_{(3, 205)} = 5.85, p < 0.01]$
Time Zone	14% for NACO Only 52% for Jeppesen Only $[F_{(1, 139)} = 27.6, p < 0.001]$	14% for VFR Pilots 45% for IFR Pilots $[F_{(1, 200)} = 26.2, p < 0.001]$	13% for < 1 Hr Flight 24% for 1 to 3 Hr Flight 52% for 3 to 6 Hr Flight 44% for 6+ Hr Flight $[F_{(3, 195)} = 4.75, p < 0.01]$
Flight Information Region (FIR)	7% for NACO Only 50% for Jeppesen Only $[F_{(1, 134)} = 44.8, p < 0.001]$	7% for VFR Pilots 47% for IFR Pilots $[F_{(1, 199)} = 47.4, p < 0.001]$	8% for < 1 Hr Flight 17% for 1 to 3 Hr Flight 50% for 3 to 6 Hr Flight 78% for 6+ Hr Flight $[F_{(3, 194)} = 17.3, p < 0.001]$
ARTCC	22% for NACO Only 8% for Jeppesen Only $[F_{(1, 165)} = 4.89, p < 0.05]$	NS	NS
Communications	0% for NACO Only 36% for Jeppesen Only $[F_{(1, 167)} = 64.4, p < 0.001]$	0% for VFR Pilots 34% for IFR Pilots $[F_{(1, 243)} = 67.3, p < 0.001]$	0% for < 1 Hr Flight 7% for 1 to 3 Hr Flight 49% for 3 to 6 Hr Flight 44% for 6+ Hr Flight $[F_{(3, 236)} = 23.0, p < 0.001]$
ADIZ Option 2 (Jeppesen/Lido)	3% for NACO Only 38% for Jeppesen Only $[F_{(1, 169)} = 43.4, p < 0.001]$	4% for VFR Pilots 28% for IFR Pilots $[F_{(1, 241)} = 30.1, p < 0.001]$	0% for < 1 Hr Flight 6% for 1 to 3 Hr Flight 46% for 3 to 6 Hr Flight 44% for 6+ Hr Flight $[F_{(3, 234)} = 23.5, p < 0.001]$

The effects of chart experience can be examined from the perspective of whether familiarity with a particular chart type affected recognition of linear patterns that were originally from that chart type. In other words, if the source of the pattern was Chart Type X, did *exclusive* users of Chart Type X recognize the pattern better than exclusive users of Chart Type Y? For this analysis, only exclusive Jeppesen and NACO chart users were considered.

Based on an examination of the source of the patterns shown in Table 11 above, the following hypotheses were posed:

- Jeppesen chart users should recognize the Time Zone linear pattern, which is used on Jeppesen charts, better than NACO chart users who do not see that pattern.

- Jeppesen chart users should recognize the FIR linear pattern, which is used on Jeppesen charts, better than NACO chart users who see a different pattern.

- NACO chart users should recognize the ARTCC linear pattern, which they are already familiar with, better than Jeppesen chart users who see a different pattern for the ARTCC.

- Jeppesen chart users should recognize the Communications boundary linear pattern, which is used on Jeppesen charts, better than NACO chart users who do not see that pattern.

- Jeppesen chart users should recognize ADIZ Option 2, which is shown on Jeppesen and Lido charts, better than NACO chart users, who are used to seeing a different pattern on their charts.

As detailed in the Chart Experience column of Table 30 (Exclusive Jeppesen vs. Exclusive NACO Users), the statistical analyses confirm all of these hypotheses, indicating that prior exposure to the linear pattern does aid in recognition.

An additional finding related to chart experience is that NACO users recognize the ADIZ linear pattern from ICAO better than Jeppesen users. Figure 4 below shows the ADIZ patterns in use by ICAO, NACO, and Jeppesen/Lido. The NACO ADIZ pattern is more similar to the ICAO pattern, so it is not surprising that NACO users recognized the ICAO ADIZ pattern.

ADIZ Option 1 (ICAO)	NACO ADIZ	ADIZ Option 2 (Jeppesen/Lido)

Figure 4. ICAO, NACO, and Jeppesen/Lido versions of the ADIZ linear pattern

Results for the IFR Pilot versus VFR Pilot analysis largely parallel those from the chart type experience after taking into consideration the positive correlation between using Jeppesen charts and being an IFR Pilot. The differences are only in the responses to the International boundary and the ARTCC. As mentioned earlier, the accuracy of recognizing the International boundary was somewhat confounded by the use of the term "state," so the results here are not conclusive. The accuracy of recognizing the ARTCC linear pattern was not significantly different between IFR and VFR Pilots, though it was between exclusive users of Jeppesen and NACO charts. This shift may be because many pilots who used multiple charts were included in the IFR and VFR Pilot analysis, but excluded from the Jeppesen versus NACO chart users analysis.

The results for the ANOVA based on Flight Length are somewhat more complex to report because there are four groups to compare instead of two (i.e., flight length less than one hour, between one to three hours, three to six hours, or longer than six hours). However, recall from the correlation matrix (Table 12) that VFR Pilots tended to fly shorter flights. In particular, many of the VFR Pilots flew one to three hour flights. Once this correlation is considered, the results from the Flight Length ANOVA are seen to once again parallel results from the other two ANOVAs. Pilots who flew the shorter flight lengths, who tend to

27

be VFR Pilots using NACO charts, recognized the ADIZ linear pattern from ICAO better. Pilots who flew longer flights, who tended to be IFR Pilots using Jeppesen charts, tended to recognize the linear patterns for the FIR, Time Zone, Communications, and the ADIZ Option 2 (Jeppesen/Lido) better.

3.4 Subjective Questions

In the Subjective Questions, pilots were asked to think of a typical flight, categorize its purpose (Air Transport, Private, Business/Corporate, or Military) and list some specific lines that are important for this typical flight. In addition, subjects responded to three questions on a numerical scale (from 1, low to 7, high), regarding the importance of lines, the difficulty of interpreting lines on paper charts, and the difficulty of interpreting lines on electronic charts. Free-response comments regarding the difficulties with paper and electronic displays, and the study and topic in general were also solicited.

The results show that four types of important lines were mentioned most often: Controlled Airspace (e.g., Class B, C, D), SUA Boundaries (e.g., Restricted, Prohibited), Route information (e.g., airways and published procedures), and Geographic information (e.g., water bodies, roads, city patterns). These items match well with the results of the Line Sorting task.

Statistical analyses of the numerical ratings are presented in Sections 3.4.1 through 3.4.3, and summarized in Section 3.4.4. Pilot comments on lines and linear patterns and on the study in general are presented in Section 3.4.5.

3.4.1 Line Importance

VFR Pilots rated lines as more *important* to them than IFR Pilots (5.46 versus 4.80) [$F(1, 260) = 9.21$, $p < 0.01$)]. In addition, the purpose for their typical flight (Air Transport, Private, Business/Corporate, or Military) significantly affected the ratings of line importance [$F(3, 251) = 4.22$, $p < 0.01$]. Paired comparison tests showed that pilots who conduct Private operations rate lines as more important than pilots who conduct Air Transport operations (5.47 versus 4.68, $p < 0.05$).

3.4.2 Difficulty of Interpreting Lines on Paper Charts versus Electronic Displays

Overall, the mean rating of difficulty for interpreting lines on paper charts, 2.90, was higher than the mean rating of difficulty for interpreting lines on electronic displays, 2.63 [$t(243) = 2.38$, $p < 0.05$]. This finding was consistent regardless of the type of operation flown, and regardless of whether the pilots were qualified for VFR operations only, or IFR operations. The difficulties of using paper charts were elaborated upon in the subjective comments, many of which were about the density of information on the paper charts. In general, electronic displays depicting aeronautical charting information provided less information than paper charts, and were therefore seen as easier to interpret.

3.4.3 Difficulty of Interpreting Lines on Electronic Displays of Charting Information

Although the electronic displays had lower subjectively reported difficulty ratings than paper charts, there were differences in the ratings for using electronic displays among different pilot groups. IFR Pilots rated the difficulties of using electronic displays lower than VFR Pilots overall (2.42 versus 2.82 [$F(1, 243) = 4.99$, $p < 0.05$].

The purpose of the flight (Air Transport, Private, Business/Corporate, or Military) significantly affected the ratings of difficulty with electronic displays [$F(3, 233) = 10.48$, $p < 0.001$]. Paired comparison tests showed that the Military pilots had the highest problem rating for electronic displays (4.25, $p < 0.05$); this was significantly higher than Air Transport (1.97), Private (2.90), and Business/Corporate operators (2.52). However, there were only eight pilots in the Military pilot group, so the sample size is small in comparison with the other groups. There were 60 Air Transport pilots, 142 Private pilots, and 27 Business/Corporate pilots in the sample.

Another finding is that the ratings of difficulty with electronic displays were significantly different ($p < 0.05$) between the Air Transport pilots (1.97) and Private pilots (2.90). This result may be underlying explanation for the result that IFR Pilot ratings reported less difficulty with lines on electronic displays than the VFR Pilots. Many of the the electronic displays used by the Air Transport pilots are navigation displays, which have a different intended function than the electronic displays typically used by Private pilots (e.g., hand held map displays, or installed multi-function displays).

3.4.4   Summary and Discussion of Subjective Rating Questions

The highlights of the subjective ratings can be summarized as follows:

1) Pilots who conduct Private operations rate lines as more important than pilots who conduct Air Transport operations.

2) Pilots of all types report that lines are harder to interpret on paper charts than electronic displays. This is likely to be because paper charts provide more information about airspaces and boundaries than common electronic displays of aeronautical charting information, such as navigation displays.

3) IFR Pilots rated the difficulties of using electronic displays lower than VFR Pilots overall. In particular, Private pilots (who tend to be in the VFR group) rated electronic displays of aeronautical information more difficult to use for interpreting lines than Air Transport pilots (who are part of the IFR group).

Note that the electronic displays that Private pilots use, such as hand-held map displays, may have different intended functions than the flight deck displays used by Air Transport pilots. In particular, navigation displays used by Air Transport pilots are simpler in terms of lines and linear patterns because they do not provide as much linear information about airspaces and boundaries; it is expected that Air Transport users with navigation displays will have supplementary information available from paper charts or electronic versions of paper charts.

There are other potential explanations for these findings as well. For example, pilots flying IFR operations, with an IFR clearance from Air Traffic Control, tend to assume that their clearance has been coordinated appropriately, so they are not as concerned about transitioning through different airspaces and boundaries. In other words, they do not *use* the linear information on the flight deck display as much when flying IFR operations, so they do not rate it as important. On the other side of the spectrum, it may be a greater design challenge to design for Private pilots precisely because more lines are more important to them, and so more linear information must be available on the display. Hence, the importance of the lines and the difficulty of using the electronic displays designed for Private pilots may be correlated.

3.4.5   Pilot Comments on Difficulties with Paper Charts and Electronic Displays

Pilots submitted hundreds of comments regarding lines and linear patterns on paper charts and electronic displays of charting information. They also submitted several comments on the topic area and study in general. An attempt was made to analyze the comments by coding each one in terms of the topic(s) it addressed. However, the analysis of comments was highly subjective.

There are a number of reasons why it is difficult to code the comments into topic areas. Some comments were unclear, or generic, and could not be coded at all (e.g., "they are generally pretty good"). Other comments could be interpreted different ways by different people. Some comments addressed multiple topics. And, a number of comments brought up system-specific problems that did not address broad topics (e.g., on this display there is the following problem…).

It was also difficult to construct a satisfactory list of comment topic areas that were independent of one another. For example, the topic of display clutter is highly correlated with the amount of information conveyed. That is, some regions are actually more complex to depict than others, so clutter is difficult if not impossible to avoid, especially on paper charts that show all information available. Display clutter is also somewhat correlated with legibility. For example, if lines overlap, the display becomes both cluttered and illegible. Even topic areas that appear to be clear-cut at first (e.g., color issues) become difficult to code in practice because the comments often express opposing points of view about the issue (e.g., "colors very helpful" versus "I have a color deficiency, so shapes are very important to me").

Table 31 shows the final list of topics that was constructed after several iterations. Example comments for each of the topic areas are also provided. Topics at the top of the table (system specific issues, etc.) received the most comments, and topics at the bottom of the table had the fewest comments (issues related to flight operation).

Table 31. Topics and examples of subjective comments.

Topic	Example Comments
System-specific issues	"30 NM radius on Class B airspace is sometimes not dark enough"
Display clutter and information density	"clutter in north east United States"
Paper versus electronic medium issues	"Folded charts hide certain symbols in the 'crease' of the fold" "You can zoom and select/de-select on an EFB, which allows a 'declutter' mode; making it easier to read"
Color	"color helps"
Legibility	"too small"
Legends	"Legend on chart is invaluable!" "Legends describing line types are hard to find or difficult to access"
Labels	"Most are self explanatory if accompanied by some kind of text" "Labels may not be visible"
Frequency of use	"Lines not referred to regularly on unfamiliar routes" "Lines which are not frequently used can be difficult to recall their meaning"
Study	"The line pattern questions were kind of pointless. Unless the lines are presented in context, it is hard to know what they are or what they represent." "Questions seem to be more for professional pilots, not GA private pilots flying VFR"
Context	"Although I didn't realize it until I took this survey, I do not rely on line types. I use position, color and shape of the line to determine its meaning."
Operations in nighttime/low light	"Colors hard to see at night on paper charts"
Issues related to flight operation (IFR vs. VFR)	"Because I'm mostly "high" altitude and IFR, I rarely am concerned about the lines on the charts or maps."

Some of the system-specific comments are particularly interesting in the context of this research. For example, although this study found that airspace information was considered to be broadly useful, a VFR pilot pointed out that he/she had to "remember to configure the instrument to show Class B, C, D lines." In other words, this pilot's display required extra steps to show information that was used often. A second VFR pilot pointed out that on his/her display "Class D, Class E, MOA's and warning areas: look alike except for color difference; poor for night flying." This display uses color as the sole difference between lines, and that does not automatically ensure that they are easy to interpret. Also, even though airport airspaces and special use airspace are both considered very useful, they should be easy to distinguish from each other.

Several pilots expressed frustration at the format of the line patterns recognition task, where they were asked to identify linear patterns without context or color. This is reflected in the difficulty of the task, which was established by the high rates of missing and Can't Tell responses, as discussed earlier in this report (Section 3.3 and Table 19). However, several pilots also indicated that they valued standardization of symbols, lines, and linear patterns and were happy to contribute their time and effort towards this goal by participating in the study.

4   Summary and Discussion

The purpose of this study was to understand what lines and linear patterns are important to pilots, and to understand whether there are some linear patterns that are currently well recognized. Data were obtained from a large sample of pilots (273) with a broad range of flight experience. Pilots completed three tasks. First they sorted a set of 65 lines and linear patterns in terms of their usefulness and familiarity. Next, they attempted to identify nine linear patterns that were presented in isolation. Finally, they answered a few subjective questions about lines on paper charts and electronic displays.

Results of the Line Sorting task identified lines and linear patterns that were very useful to most pilots, very useful to some pilots, somewhat useful to most pilots, or not recognized/used by many pilots. There were clearly some items that were only useful to specific pilot groups. The full results of this task may be used by the SAE G-10 Aeronautical Charting Committee to determine which lines and linear patterns should be assigned specific recommendations in the updated ARP 5289A industry recommendations document. For example, recommendations may be most useful for the items considered important to IFR and VFR Pilots listed in Table 13, such as the different Airspace Classes, and Prohibited/Restricted Areas. Authorities can use either the full results of this study, or the ARP 5289A document to evaluate whether the information needs of the pilots are met by various displays.

The results of the Line Sorting task can also be used by manufacturers to determine what lines and linear patterns would be useful to pilots given a particular type of flight operation. For example, manufacturers of displays for Private pilots should consider the results for the Private VFR, Private IFR, and Private Business operators together. Manufacturers of displays for both Air Transport and Corporate operations should consider the needs of both groups individually as well.

Results of the Linear Patterns Recognition task may be used in identifying whether some linear patterns are currently well recognized, and should be recommended for use as is. Recognizing linear patterns in isolation was a difficult task, and overall, recognition rates were relatively low, particularly in comparison to the recognition rates obtained for identifying specific symbols such as the navigation aid symbols and other general symbols that were evaluated in Chandra & Yeh, 2007. The most recognizable linear pattern was the Special Use Airspace boundary, which obtained a 51% recognition rate, whereas navigation aid symbols were typically recognized by pilots 80% of the time, or better. Although the recognition rates for linear patterns were relatively low overall, some patterns were better recognized than others and these results may be used by the SAE G-10 Aeronautical Charting Committee to determine which linear patterns should be included in the recommendations document. Even if the linear pattern is not recognized by a majority of pilots, reusing an existing symbol will aid pilots who are familiar with it, and it may reduce future potential conflicts with that symbol.

Data on recognition rate is only available for a few linear patterns, so most of the recommendations in SAE ARP 5289A will be based on the pilot ratings of utility from the Line Sorting task. However, results of the Line Sorting task and Linear Patterns Recognition task can also be used jointly to develop recommendations as shown in Table 32 below.

For example, if an item is rated as very useful in the sorting task, and a linear pattern for that item had a good recognition rate, then a recommendation to use that particular linear pattern is reasonable. This was the case with the Special Use Airspace boundary (used to represent Prohibited and Restricted airspace areas) and the Controlled Airspace boundary (used to represent Class B, C, and D airspace). Both of these were identified as very useful by IFR and VFR Pilots, and had relatively high recognition rates (51% and 43% respectively).

If an item is rated as not recognized/useful, and a linear pattern for that item was not well recognized, then no recommendation is needed. This was the case with the ARTCC linear pattern, which was designated by pilots as not very useful and had a relatively poorly recognition rate of just 18%. When a linear pattern *is* recognized, even moderately, a recommendation to use that pattern should be considered when the item is *very* or even *somewhat* useful. For example, the Time Zone linear pattern was identified as somewhat useful by most pilots and it had a moderate rate of recognition (30%). The pattern could be recommended in order to avoid the development of linear patterns inconsistent with it and in order to avoid the use of that pattern to represent a different aeronautical element.

When using these data jointly, keep in mind that the utility ratings varied by pilot group, and the different pilot group ratings may need to be considered, not just the aggregate utility rating across all pilots. For example, the FIR linear pattern was not considered to be very useful by either IFR or VFR Pilots and had only moderate recognition across all pilots (28%). However, it was identified as very useful by Air Transport, International, and long haul pilots and had a high recognition rate within these groups; 78% of pilots who fly long flights recognized the FIR linear pattern. As such, it may make sense to recommend the tested FIR pattern.

Table 32. Suggestions for using the line sorting data and linear pattern recognition data jointly.

Line Sorting Task Utility Rating	Linear Pattern Recognition Task Recognition Rate Relative to Other Tested Patterns.		
	Good	Moderate	Poor
Very Useful	Recommend use of the tested linear pattern.	Consider making a recommendation to use the tested linear pattern to avoid confusion and retraining.	Consider making a recommendation, but no linear pattern is suggested.
Recognize/Use on Occasion	Consider making a recommendation to use the tested linear pattern to avoid confusion and retraining.	Consider making a recommendation to use the tested linear pattern to avoid confusion and retraining.	Recommendation to use the tested linear pattern may not be necessary
Do Not Use/Do Not Recognize	No recommendation needed. Suggestion is available.	No recommendation needed. Suggestion is available.	No recommendation needed. No linear pattern suggested.

Finally, results from the subjective questions about lines found that pilots do find it difficult to interpret lines on paper charts for a variety of reasons. The interpretation of lines on electronic displays that depict aeronautical charting information is somewhat less problematic, but this is probably because these displays show only a subset of the information available on paper charts. As electronic displays are developed with the intended function of replacing paper charts, the issues of information density will become more important.

5   Conclusions

This report describes a study conducted to explore the utility and recognition of lines and linear patterns on electronic displays depicting aeronautical charting information. The results of this study provide valuable information for the development of an industry recommendations document that will help manufacturers and authorities assess whether the information needs of the pilots are met by various displays. In order to maximize the applicability of the results, data were collected from pilots who fly all types of operations, all around the world. Items that were useful to different pilot groups were identified based on pilot qualifications, types of flight operations, and typical flight length. Recognition of a test set of nine linear patterns was difficult, but some patterns were more recognizable than others.

Results of this study will be considered in the development of an updated industry recommendations document, specifically, the SAE International document on Electronic Aeronautical Symbols (ARP 5289A). The Federal Aviation Administration or the International Civil Aviation Organization may choose to adopt this industry document by reference. Note that this research applies to any electronic display that shows the lines and linear patterns tested in this study, regardless of the intended function of the display.

6   References

Chandra, D. C and M. Yeh (2007). *Pilot Identification of Symbols and an Exploration of Symbol Design Issues for Electronic Displays of Aeronautical Charting Information* (Report Nos. DOT/FAA/AR-07/37, DOT-VNTSC-FAA-07-07). Cambridge, MA, US DOT Volpe National Transportation Systems Center.

Chandra, D.C., Yeh, M. and C.M. Donovan (2007). Pilot Identification of Proposed Electronic Symbols for Displays for Aeronautical Charting Information. In Proceedings of the 51st Annual Meeting of the Human Factors and Ergonomics Society. Santa Monica, CA: Human Factors and Ergonomics Society. pp. 65-69.

Federal Aviation Administration (2007a). *Instrument procedures handbook* (FAA-H-8261-1A). Washington, DC: Author.

Federal Aviation Administration (2007b). *Federal Aviation Regulations/Aeronautical information manual* (ASA-07-FR-AM-8K). Newcastle, WA: Aviation Supplies & Academics.

Society of Automotive Engineers (SAE) (1997). *Electronic Aeronautical Symbols*, ARP 5289. Warrendale, PA, SAE.

Yeh, M. and D. C. Chandra (2005). *Designing and Evaluating Symbols for Electronic Displays of Navigation Information: Symbol Stereotypes and Symbol-Feature Rules.* (Report Nos. DOT/FAA/AR-05/48, DOT-VNTSC-FAA-05-16) Cambridge, MA, US DOT Volpe National Transportation Systems Center.

Yeh, M. and D.C. Chandra (2006). Pilot stereotypes for navigation symbols on electronic displays. In Reuzeau, F., Corker, K. & Boy, G. (Eds.) Proceedings of the International Conference on Human-Computer Interaction in Aeronautics. (pp. 66-73). Toulouse, France: Cépaduès-Éditions.

Yeh, M. and D.C. Chandra, (2008) *Survey of Symbology for Aeronautical Charts and Electronic Displays: Navigation Aids, Airports, Lines, and Linear Patterns.* (Report Nos. DOT/FAA/AR-07/66, DOT-VNTSC-FAA-08-01) Cambridge, MA, US DOT Volpe National Transportation Systems Center.

Appendix A: Survey Materials (Fall 2007 Version)

USDOT Volpe Center Flight Symbology Human Factors Study
Fall 2007

Principal Investigator:	Divya Chandra, US DOT Volpe Center, chandra@volpe.dot.gov, 617.494.3882
Associate Investigator:	Michelle Yeh, US DOT Volpe Center, yeh@volpe.dot.gov, 617.494.3459
Research Sponsor:	Federal Aviation Administration Human Factors Research and Engineering Group Tom McCloy, Program Manager

Overview

The United States Department of Transportation (USDOT) John A. Volpe National Transportation Systems Center (Volpe Center), located in Cambridge, Massachusetts, is conducting a human-factors study on electronic symbols for charting information on flight deck displays.

The study examines how pilots use lines shown on moving-map displays and/or electronic charts (e.g., boundaries, such as "Class B airspace"). More specifically, the tasks explore which lines are of high utility, what current linear patterns are well recognized, and how pilots use lines in general.

Active pilots who only fly VFR operations are requested to participate in the study.

Outcomes

The results of this study will be used to help produce national and international recommendations for lines shown on moving maps and electronic charts via the SAE International G-10 Aeronautical Charting Committee. This committee is developing industry recommendations for electronic chart and map displays. The final results will also be available to the public in a published government report.

Reports on this and related research are available at www.volpe.dot.gov/hf under the publications section.

Instructions for Flight Symbology Study

The study is expected to take 30 to 45 minutes to complete. The steps are listed below.

1) Informed Consent Form (1 page)

   Please read the informed consent form and sign at the bottom. By signing this document, you indicate to us that you voluntarily consent to participate in the study. The form also assures you that your participation is strictly confidential.

   Questionnaires returned without a signed consent form cannot be considered. Keep in mind that your confidentiality is assured even after signing the consent form, because it will be separated from your responses upon receipt.

2) Background Questionnaire (1 page)

   Please fill this out so that we know a bit about your flight experience.

3) Specific Tasks

   a. Line Sorting Task
      (1 page of Instructions, 2 titled pieces of paper, and 3 sheets with pre-printed labels)
      See Instructions at the beginning of the task.

   b. Line Patterns Questionnaire (2 pages, 10 questions total)
      See Instructions at the beginning of the task.

   c. Subjective Questions about Lines on Chart/Map Displays (1 page)
      Please respond to a few open-ended questions about your use of lines on charts and map displays.

4) After completing study, please mail back all the materials (including unused labels) in the **pre-addressed** envelope by **JANUARY 7, 2008** to:

   Divya Chandra/Michelle Yeh
   USDOT Volpe Center
   Human Factors Division, RTV-4G
   55 Broadway
   Cambridge, MA 02142   (USA)

You may keep the overview sheet with our contact information if you like.

Thank you very much for your help with this study!

Flight Symbology Research Project
US DOT Volpe Center
Informed Consent

I, _____, understand that this study, entitled "Flight Symbology" is being conducted by the Volpe National Transportation Systems Center, United States Department of Transportation, and is being directed by Dr. Divya Chandra. This research is funded by the Federal Aviation Administration, Human Factors Research and Engineering Group.

Purpose of Study. There are many types of electronic displays that show navigation information to help pilots determine the aircraft's position. There are no standards in widespread use that ensure the compatibility of the symbols across all the various display platforms. The purpose of this study is to understand which line patterns are most useful and whether certain line patterns are recognizable.

Study Procedures. There are three parts to the study. First, you will also be given a list of lines and asked to sort them into categories based on their utility. Second, you will be shown a set of line patterns and asked to identify them. Finally, we ask a few questions about your use of lines. The whole study is estimated to take less than 45 minutes to complete.

Discomfort and Risks. The risks involved in your participation are low and do not exceed those you would experience working at your desk.

Benefits to You. Participation provides an opportunity to aid in the development of recommendations for the design of air transport and general aviation displays.

Participant Responsibilities. Please notify Dr. Divya Chandra (617-494-3882) if you experience any discomfort during the study.

In the Event of an Injury, we urge that you report any immediate or delayed injuries resulting from the study to Dr. Divya Chandra (617-494-3882).

Assurances and Rights of the Participant. Your participation in this study is completely voluntary. Your participation is strictly confidential, and no individual names or identities will be recorded with any data or released in any reports. Only arbitrary numbers are used to identify pilots who provide data. You may terminate your participation in the study at any time.

If you have any questions, please let us know. For further information about this study, please feel free to contact:

Divya Chandra or Michelle Yeh
US DOT Volpe Center, 55 Broadway, Cambridge, MA 02142
617.494.3882 / 617.494.3459
chandra, yeh@volpe.dot.gov

Statement of Consent

I have read this consent document. I understand its contents, and I freely consent to participate in this study under the conditions described. I may have a copy of this consent form if I request same.

Research Participant: _____ Date: _____

Background Questionnaire

Age (circle one)   **30 or under**   **31 to 60**   **61 or over**

Flight Hours   Total _____   Average (per month) _____

Last month _____

Instrument Time Total _____   Average (per month) _____

Last month _____

Ratings and Certificates: Please check the ratings and certificates that you have.

Private Pilot Only (VFR) _____   Air Transport _____   Commercial _____

Instrument _____   Multi-Engine _____   Rotorcraft _____

Flight Experience: Please check the type(s) of flying that you do most frequently.

Private IFR _____   Private Business _____   Air transport _____   International _____

Private VFR _____   Corporate _____   Military _____   FAA/Regulatory _____

What is the typical length of a recent flight? (circle one)

Under 1 hour   1 to 3 hours   3 to 6 hours   Longer than 6 hours

Describe the region where you typically fly (e.g., country/state(s), typical origin/destination)

Avionics Experience: Please check whether you have experience with the following systems.

Glass cockpit _____   If yes, which type aircraft are you most familiar with? _____

Moving Map Displays _____   If yes, which model are you most familiar with? _____

Traffic Displays _____   TCAS I   TCAS II   Mode S TIS   Capstone/TIS-B
(circle one or write-in)   Other (specify) _____

Chart Experience

Which charts do you use most?   _____ Jeppesen
How long have you used these charts?   _____ US Government (NACO/DoD)
_____ LIDO
_____   _____ Other (specify)

Other charts you use regularly?   _____ None
How long have you used these charts?   _____ Jeppesen
_____ US Government (NACO/DoD)
_____   _____ LIDO
_____ Other (specify)

A.5

Line Sorting Task Instructions

Please sort the 65 items described on the pre-printed labels into <u>three</u> categories by completing the following steps.

First, familiarize yourself with the **titles** on each sheet of paper.

Next, review the **pre-printed labels** and look for items that are familiar to you. There are 30 (1-30) items on the first sheet, 30 (30-60) on the second sheet, and 5 (61-65) on the last sheet. Please be sure to look over all 65 items. (Note that the numbers on the labels are only for us to use in recording the responses. You can ignore them.)

One at a time, remove and sort labels for items that are familiar to you. Place the labels onto one of the two titled sheets of paper accordingly. The sequence in which items are placed on the two sheets of paper is not important. (If you change your mind after sticking the label, simply write a note on the label where it should go instead.)

Base your label-sorting decisions on the following criteria:

(a) *Items that I find to be **very useful in general**.* These are items that you know well and refer to frequently. They should be easily identifiable. Place these items on the first sheet of paper.

(b) *Items that I **recognize and use on occasion**.* These are items that you use on occasion, but not as frequently as those you would place on the other sheet of paper. Place these items on the second sheet of paper.

(c) *Items that I **do not commonly use, or I do not recognize**.* These are items that you seldom use, or you are not sure of their meaning and need more information in order to understand their use. <u>Leave these items on their original label sheet.</u>

A.6

Line Sorting Task

Items that I find to be **very useful in general**.
These are items that you know well and refer to frequently. They need to be easily identifiable.

Line Sorting Task

Items that I **recognize and use on occasion**.
These are items that you use on occasion, but not as frequently as those you would place on the other sheet of paper.

1 Air Defense Identification Zones (ADIZ)	**11** City Pattern	**21** Control Area CTA/CTL
2 Air Route Traffic Control Center (ARTCC)	**12** Class A Airspace	**22** Control Zone / Air Traffic Zone (CTR/CTZ/ATZ)
3 Airport Radar Service Area (ARSA)	**13** Class B Airspace	**23** Controlled Firing Area (CFA) (United States)
4 Alert Areas (A)	**14** Class C Airspace	**24** Country (State) Boundary
5 Alternate, Conditional or Uncontrolled Enroute Airway or ATS Route	**15** Class D Airspace	**25** Danger Areas (D)
6 Altimeter Setting Regions (QFE/QNH)	**16** Class E Airspace	**26** Enroute Airway or ATS Route
7 Balloon Launch Area	**17** Class F Airspace	**27** Enroute ATC Holding Pattern
8 Bluff	**18** Class G Airspace	**28** Flight Information Region / Upper Flight Information Region (FIR/UIR)
9 Buffer Zone / Non-Free Flying Zone	**19** CNS/ATM Equipment Requirement Areas (RNP, RVSM, MNPS, Mode C, etc.)	**29** Formation Radial or Bearing (Enroute & Terminal)
10 Caution Areas (C)	**20** Contours	**30** Helicopter Traffic Zone / Protected Zone (HTZ/HPZ)

A.9

31	41	51
International Date Line	Prohibited Airspace Area (P)	Telephone or Power Lines
32	**42**	**52**
Isogonic Lines	Radar Vector Track	Temporary Flight Restriction Area (TFR)
33	**43**	**53**
Lake or Pond	Railroad (single or multiple track)	Temporary Reserve/ Segregated Areas (European equivalent of MOA)
34	**44**	**54**
Military Control Zone / Military Air Traffic Zone (MCTR/MATZ)	Restricted Airspace Area (R)	Terminal ATC Holding Pattern
35	**45**	**55**
Military Operations Area (MOA)	River or Stream	Terminal Control Area (TCA/TMA)
36	**46**	**56**
Missed Approach Procedure Holding Pattern	Road (single or multi-lane)	Terminal Procedure Course Reversal Holding Pattern
37	**47**	**57**
Missed Approach Procedure Track	Shoreline	Terminal Procedure Flight Track
38	**48**	**58**
National Security Area (NSA) (United States)	Special Rules Area / Zone (SRA/SRZ)	Terminal Radar Service Area (TRSA)
39	**49**	**59**
Oceanic Control Area (OCA)	Special VFR NA (Fixed Wing) Airspace	Terminal Transition or Feeder Route (Arrival, Departure, Approach)
40	**50**	**60**
Positive Control Area (PCA)	Speed Limit Area	Time Zone Boundary

61
Traffic Information Area/Zone (TIA/TIZ)
62
Training Areas (T)
63
Upper Control Area (UCA/UTA)
64
Visual Flight Track
65
Warning Areas (W)

Line Pattern Questionnaire

The purpose of this task is to determine whether line patterns being proposed for use on electronic charts are well recognized. For each line pattern below, try to identify it and indicate the level of confidence in your response. Some of the line patterns are unusual, so you should not expect to be familiar with them all. Write "?" if you do not know what the line pattern represents.

Note that the patterns are drawn in black and white here, but they may be shown in color on an actual chart. Please disregard the lack of color.

1. ⎍⎍⎍⎍⎍⎍⎍⎍	Line pattern (or ?): _____ 1　　2　　3　　4　　5　　6　　7 Low　　　　Medium　　　　High Confidence　Confidence　Confidence
2. (pattern)	Line pattern (or ?): _____ 1　　2　　3　　4　　5　　6　　7 Low　　　　Medium　　　　High Confidence　Confidence　Confidence
3. //////////////	Line pattern (or ?): _____ 1　　2　　3　　4　　5　　6　　7 Low　　　　Medium　　　　High Confidence　Confidence　Confidence
4. :::::::::::::::::::::::	Line pattern (or ?): _____ 1　　2　　3　　4　　5　　6　　7 Low　　　　Medium　　　　High Confidence　Confidence　Confidence
5. ××××××××××××	Line pattern (or ?): _____ 1　　2　　3　　4　　5　　6　　7 Low　　　　Medium　　　　High Confidence　Confidence　Confidence

Line Pattern Questionnaire (continued)

6.	Line pattern (or ?): _____ 1 2 3 4 5 6 7 Low Medium High Confidence Confidence Confidence
7.	Line pattern (or ?): _____ 1 2 3 4 5 6 7 Low Medium High Confidence Confidence Confidence
8.	Line pattern (or ?): _____ 1 2 3 4 5 6 7 Low Medium High Confidence Confidence Confidence
9.	Line pattern (or ?): _____ 1 2 3 4 5 6 7 Low Medium High Confidence Confidence Confidence
10.	Line pattern (or ?): _____ 1 2 3 4 5 6 7 Low Medium High Confidence Confidence Confidence

Subjective Questions about Lines on Chart/Map Displays

1) Describe a typical flight operation for you.

Origin: _____   Destination: _____

Purpose of Flight (circle one)

    Air Transport   Military   Business/Corporate   Private

How important would <u>lines on charts/maps</u> be to you during this typical flight?

1	2	3	4	5	6	7
Low			Medium			High
Importance			Importance			Importance

List up to three specific lines that are important to you during this flight. (Review the list of line types from the Sorting Task, if needed.)

    a) _____

    b) _____

    c) _____

2) How often do you have difficulty interpreting lines on <u>paper charts</u>?

1	2	3	4	5	6	7
Rarely			Sometimes			Frequently

Please provide any comments/examples about the difficulty of interpreting lines on paper charts.

3) How often do you have difficulty interpreting lines on <u>electronic charts and map displays</u>?

1	2	3	4	5	6	7
Rarely			Sometimes			Frequently

Please provide any comments/examples about the difficulty of interpreting lines on electronic charts and map displays.

4) Please provide any general comments you have about this study, or the general topic, lines on electronic charts and map displays.

Appendix B:
Introductory Survey Materials from Spring 2007 Version

USDOT Volpe Center Flight Symbology Human Factors Study
Spring 2007

Principal Investigator: Divya Chandra, US DOT Volpe Center, chandra@volpe.dot.gov, 617.494.3882

Associate Investigator: Michelle Yeh, US DOT Volpe Center, yeh@volpe.dot.gov, 617.494.3459

Research Sponsor: Federal Aviation Administration Human Factors Research and Engineering Group
Tom McCloy, Program Manager

Overview

The United States Department of Transportation (USDOT) John A. Volpe National Transportation Systems Center (Volpe Center), located in Cambridge, Massachusetts, is conducting a two-part human-factors study on electronic symbols used on flight deck displays.

The first part of the study examines how pilots use lines shown on moving-map displays and/or electronic charts (e.g., boundaries, such as "Class B airspace"). More specifically, the tasks explore which lines are of high utility, what current line patterns are well recognized, and how pilots use lines in general.

The second part of the study addresses new symbols that are being proposed to depict other aircraft in your vicinity. These symbols can convey detailed information about other aircraft via Automatic Dependent Surveillance-Broadcast (ADS-B). This study explores how intuitive the proposed traffic symbols are.

Active instrument-rated pilots are requested to participate in the study. Any type of flight experience is acceptable.

Outcomes

The results of this study will be used to help produce national and international recommendations on traffic-display symbols and lines on moving maps and electronic charts. Results of the tasks pertaining to lines will be used by the SAE International G-10 Aeronautical Charting Committee in developing industry recommendations for electronic chart and map displays. Results of the tasks pertaining to traffic-display symbology will be used by the RTCA Special Committee 186, on Cockpit Displays of Traffic Information. The results will also be available to the public in a published government report.

Reports on this and related research are available at www.volpe.dot.gov/hf under the publications section.

(4/5/07)

Instructions for Flight Symbology Study

The study is expected to take 45 to 60 minutes to complete. The steps are listed below.

1) Informed Consent Form (1 page)

   Please read the informed consent form and sign at the bottom. By signing this document, you indicate to us that you voluntarily consent to participate in the study. The form also assures you that your participation is strictly confidential.

   Questionnaires returned without a signed consent form cannot be considered. Keep in mind that your confidentiality is assured even after signing the consent form, because it will be separated from your responses upon receipt.

2) Background Questionnaire (1 page)

   Please fill this out so that we know a bit about your flight experience.

3) Part 1: Lines
   a. Line Sorting Task
      (1 page of Instructions, 2 titled pieces of paper, and 3 sheets with pre-printed labels)
         See Instructions at the beginning of the task.

   b. Line Patterns Questionnaire (2 pages, 10 questions total)
      (1 page of Instructions, 2 titled pieces of paper, and 3 sheets with pre-printed labels)
      See Instructions at the beginning of the task.

   c. Subjective Questions about Lines on Chart/Map Displays (1 page)
      Please respond to a few open-ended questions about your use of lines on charts and map displays.

4) Part 2: Traffic Symbols (3 pages)

   See the Background and Instructions at the beginning of this task.

5) After completing study, please return all the materials (including unused labels) in the pre-addressed envelope by _____ to:

   Divya Chandra/Michelle Yeh
   USDOT Volpe Center
   Human Factors Division, RTV-4G
   55 Broadway
   Cambridge, MA 02142   (USA)

You may keep the overview sheet with our contact information if you like.

Thank you very much for your help with this study!

Flight Symbology Research Project
US DOT Volpe Center
Informed Consent

I, _____, understand that this study, entitled "Flight Symbology" is being conducted by the Volpe National Transportation Systems Center, United States Department of Transportation, and is being directed by Dr. Divya Chandra. This research is funded by the Federal Aviation Administration, Human Factors Research and Engineering Group.

Purpose of Study. There are many types of electronic displays that show navigation information to help pilots determine the aircraft's position. There are no standards in widespread use that ensure the compatibility of the symbols across all the various display platforms. The purpose of the first part of this study is to understand which line patterns are most useful and whether certain line patterns are recognizable. The second part of the study examines the ease of understanding new symbols that are proposed to depict traffic information on cockpit displays.

Study Procedures. There are three parts to the line styles section of this study. First, you will also be given a list of lines and asked to sort them into categories based on their utility. Second, you will be shown a set of line patterns and asked to identify them. Finally, we ask a few questions about your use of lines. In the traffic symbol portion of the study, you will be asked to interpret the meaning of the proposed traffic symbology. The whole study is estimated to take less than one hour to complete.

Discomfort and Risks. The risks involved in your participation are low and do not exceed those you would experience working at your desk.

Benefits to You. Participation provides an opportunity to aid in the development of recommendations for the design of air transport and general aviation displays.

Participant Responsibilities. Please notify Dr. Divya Chandra (617-494-3882) if you experience any discomfort during the study.

In the Event of an Injury, we urge that you report any immediate or delayed injuries resulting from the study to Dr. Divya Chandra (617-494-3882).

Assurances and Rights of the Participant. Your participation in this study is completely voluntary. Your participation is strictly confidential, and no individual names or identities will be recorded with any data or released in any reports. Only arbitrary numbers are used to identify pilots who provide data. You may terminate your participation in the study at any time.

If you have any questions, please let us know. For further information about this study, please feel free to contact:

Divya Chandra or Michelle Yeh
US DOT Volpe Center, 55 Broadway, Cambridge, MA 02142
617.494.3882 / 617.494.3459
chandra, yeh@volpe.dot.gov

Statement of Consent

I have read this consent document. I understand its contents, and I freely consent to participate in this study under the conditions described. I may have a copy of this consent form if I request same.

Research Participant: _____Date: _____

Background Questionnaire

Age (circle one)   30 or under   31 to 60   61 or over

Flight Hours   Total _____   Average (per month) _____

                                                    Last month _____

Instrument Time Total _____   Average (per month) _____

                                                    Last month _____

Ratings and Certificates: Please check the ratings and certificates that you have.

Instrument _____   Multi-Engine _____   Rotorcraft _____

Air Transport _____   Commercial _____

Flight Experience: Please check the type(s) of flying that you do most frequently.

Private IFR ____   Private Business ____   Air transport ____   International ____

Private VFR ____   Corporate ____   Military ____   FAA/Regulatory ____

What is the typical length of a recent flight? (circle one)

      Under 1 hour   1 to 3 hours   3 to 6 hours   Longer than 6 hours

Describe the region where you typically fly (e.g., country/state(s), typical origin/destination)

Avionics Experience: Please check whether you have experience with the following systems.

Glass cockpit ____   If yes, which type aircraft are you most familiar with? _____

Moving Map Displays ____   If yes, which model are you most familiar with? _____

Traffic Displays ____   TCAS I   TCAS II   Mode S TIS   Capstone/TIS-B

(circle one or write-in)   Other (specify) _____

Chart Experience

Which charts do you use most?   ___ Jeppesen

How long have you used these charts?   ___ US Government (NACO/DoD)

      _____   ___ LIDO

                                             ___ Other (specify)

Other charts you use regularly?   ___ None

How long have you used these charts?   ___ Jeppesen

      _____   ___ US Government (NACO/DoD)

                                             ___ LIDO

                                             ___ Other (specify)

Appendix C: Item Definitions

This Appendix primarily provides definitions for lines and linear patterns that represent areas/regions and zones. One general airspace element is included – a "Special VFR NA (fixed wing)" airspace. These airspace and boundary elements may be uncommon, and in fact, some exist only in certain countries or regions.

Definitions were identified through a variety of sources. The Volpe Center worked with members of the SAE G-10 Aeronautical Charting Committee to identify key references. Additionally, the International Civil Aviation Organization (ICAO) provided a glossary of terms, and Jeppesen-Sanderson, Inc. searched various State Aeronautical Information Publications (AIPs). Definitions were extracted verbatim from the source. In some cases, text was edited so that the definition would apply more generally. For example, some definitions include lateral and vertical dimensions for an airspace or boundary, but these dimensions may not be applicable worldwide and are thus omitted here.

The source for each definition is indicated next to the item; a list of sources is provided at the end of this Appendix. Excerpted definitions are identified accordingly in the source. An FAA definition was used when possible. When no FAA definition existed, an ICAO definition was used. When neither was available, Jeppesen-Sanderson Inc. either provided a State's AIP definition or composed a definition that reflected their understanding of the particular airspace type and its usage. The definitions below are intended for general reference only; they are not an endorsement of any particular source nor do they represent a world-wide definition. The definition provided by one State may differ slightly from that of another State, and no attempt was made to compare the definitions.

Advisory Areas (Canada)	Airspace of defined dimensions within which a high volume of pilot training or an unusual type of aerial activity may be carried out. *Source: Transport Canada, Designated Airspace Handbook*
Air Defense Identification Zones (ADIZ)	The area of airspace over land or water, extending upward from the surface, within which the ready identification, the location, and the control of aircraft are required in the interest of national security. *Source: AIM Pilot/Controller Glossary*
Air Route Traffic Control Center (ARTCC)	A facility established to provide air traffic control service to aircraft operating on IFR flight plans within controlled airspace and principally during the en route phase of flight. When equipment capabilities and controller workload permit, certain advisory/assistance services may be provided to VFR aircraft. *Source: AIM Pilot/Controller Glossary*
Air Traffic Zone/Aerodrome Traffic Zone (ATZ)	An ATZ is an area of airspace that is established around civil and military airfields. Aircraft within an ATZ must obey the instructions of the tower controller (if present), or must make radio contact with the Information Officer or Air/Ground radio unit on the airport before entering the zone (in the case of an uncontrolled airfield), or must obey ground signals if non-radio. *Source: Excerpted from United Kingdom AIP*
Airport Radar Service Area (ARSA)	This term is no longer in use. It was previously used for what is now known as Class C airspace.

Alert Areas (A)	Airspace which may contain a high volume of pilot training activities or an unusual type of aerial activity, neither of which is hazardous to aircraft. Alert Areas are depicted on aeronautical charts for the information of nonparticipating pilots. All activities within an Alert Area are conducted in accordance with Federal Aviation Regulations, and pilots of participating aircraft as well as pilots transiting the area are equally responsible for collision avoidance. *Source: AIM Pilot/Controller Glossary (Special Use Airspace). See also AIM, Paragraph 3-4-6*
Altimeter Setting Regions (QFE/QNH)	QNE- The barometric pressure used for the standard altimeter setting (29.92 inches Hg.). QNH- The barometric pressure as reported by a particular station. *Source: AIM Pilot/Controller Glossary*
Balloon Launch Area	Airspace of defined dimensions within which a high volume of balloon launch or related aerial activity may be carried out. *Source: Jeppesen*
Buffer Zone/Non-Free Flying Zone	A military term which describes airspace of defined dimensions, established in an area of political unrest, international conflict, or a war zone within which civilian aircraft are not permitted to operate without prior permission of the controlling military authorities. *Source: Jeppesen*
Caution Areas	An airspace of defined dimensions within which uncontrolled and maneuvering aircraft may be encountered, so it is necessary for the pilots to use caution when entering such airspace for avoidance of danger. Pilots of participating aircraft as well as pilots transiting the area are responsible for collision avoidance and pilots transiting Caution Areas should coordinate with Air Traffic Service (ATS) units prior to entering such areas. *Source: Islamic Republic of Iran AIP*
CNS/ATM Equipment Requirement Areas (e.g. ADS-B, RVSM, MNPS, RNP, etc.)	Airspace of defined dimensions, independent from any other airspace area, where specific equipment requirements related to aircraft Communications, Navigation, Surveillance, and Air Traffic Management systems have been established by the appropriate Air Traffic Service (ATS) authority or Air Traffic Control (ATC) unit. *Source: Jeppesen*
Control Area (CTA/CTL)	A controlled airspace extending upwards from a specified limit above the earth. *Source: ICAO International Civil Aviation Vocabulary*
Control Zone (CTZ/CTR)	A controlled airspace extending upwards from the surface of the earth to a specified upper limit. *Source: ICAO International Civil Aviation Vocabulary*
Controlled Firing Area (CFA) (United States)	Airspace wherein activities are conducted under conditions so controlled as to eliminate hazards to nonparticipating aircraft and to ensure the safety of persons and property on the ground. *Source: AIM Pilot/Controller Glossary (Special Use Airspace). See also AIM Paragraph 3-4-7*

Danger Areas (D)	An airspace of defined dimensions within which activities dangerous to the flight of aircraft may exist at specified times. *Source: ICAO International Civil Aviation Vocabulary*
Flight Information Region (FIR)	An airspace of defined dimensions within which Flight Information Service and Alerting Service are provided. *Source: AIM Pilot/Controller Glossary*
Helicopter Protected Zone (HPZ)	A non-controlled airspace of defined dimensions extending upwards from sea level to a specified upper limit. An HPZ is established in order to indicate frequent helicopter activity in the area. *Source: Excerpted from Norway AIP*
Helicopter Traffic Zone (HTZ)	A non-controlled airspace of defined dimensions extending upwards from sea level to a defined upper limit. A HTZ is established around an offshore installation with landing pad. An HTZ is established in order to indicate the performance of helicopter approach and departures. *Source: Excerpted from Norway AIP*
Military Air Traffic Zone (MATZ)	At certain military aerodromes, Military Aerodrome Traffic Zones (MATZ) have been established for the increased protection of arriving, departing and circuit traffic. Additional mandatory Air Traffic Control (ATC) requirements are invariably specified for military pilots. The purpose of the MATZ is to provide a volume of airspace within which increased protection may be given to aircraft in the critical stages of circuit, approach and climb-out. *Source: United Kingdom AIP*
Military Control Zone (MCTR)	See Military Air Traffic Zone (MATZ).
Military Operations Area (MOA)	A MOA is airspace established outside of Class A airspace area to separate or segregate certain nonhazardous military activities from IFR traffic and to identify for VFR traffic where these activities are conducted. *Source: AIM Pilot/Controller Glossary (Special Use Airspace). See also AIM Paragraph 3-4-5*
Military Terminal Control Area (MTCA)	Controlled airspace of defined dimensions normally established in the vicinity of a military aerodrome and within which special procedures and exemptions exist for military aircraft. *Source: Canada Flight Supplement*
National Security Area (NSA) (United States)	National Security Areas consist of airspace of defined vertical and lateral dimensions established at locations where there is a requirement for increased security and safety of ground facilities. Pilots are requested to voluntarily avoid flying through the depicted NSA. When it is necessary to provide a greater level of security and safety, flight in NSAs may be temporarily prohibited by regulation under the provisions of 14 CFR Section 99.7. Regulatory prohibitions will be issued by System Operations, System Operations Airspace and AIM Office, Airspace and Rules, and disseminated via NOTAM. Inquiries about NSAs should be directed to Airspace and Rules. *Source: AIM 3-5-7*

Oceanic Control Area (OCA)	Airspace over the oceans of the world, considered international airspace, where ICAO oceanic separation and procedures are applied. Responsibility for the provisions of air traffic control service in this airspace is delegated to various countries, based generally upon geographic proximity and the availability of the required resources. *Source: Jeppesen*
Positive Control Area (PCA)	Any aircraft shall, under instrument meteorological conditions, be flown in accordance with instrument flight rules within an air traffic control area or an air traffic control zone, and not fly in any other airspace. *Source: Japan AIP (referencing Civil Aeronautics Law)*
Prohibited Airspace Area (P)	Airspace designated under 14 CFR Part 73 within which no person may operate an aircraft without the permission of the using agency. *Source: AIM Pilot/Controller Glossary (Special Use Airspace). See also AIM Paragraph 3-4-2*
Restricted Airspace Area (R)	Airspace designated under 14 CFR Part 73, within which the flight of aircraft, while not wholly prohibited, is subject to restriction. Most restricted areas are designated joint use and IFR/VFR operations in the area may be authorized by the controlling ATC facility when it is not being utilized by the using agency. Restricted areas are depicted on en route charts. Where joint use is authorized, the name of the ATC controlling facility is also shown. *Source: AIM Pilot/Controller Glossary (Special Use Airspace). See also AIM Paragraph 3-4-3*
Special Rules Area/Zone (SRA/SRZ)	Controlled airspace within which special rules and procedures are prescribed and published for the protection of IFR flights from VFR flights. *Source: Excerpted from Austria AIP*
Special VFR NA (Fixed Wing) Airspace (United States)	Airspace associated with Class B terminal airspace areas where Air Traffic Control (ATC)-approved special VFR clearances are not authorized (i.e., no special clearances for VFR aircraft when weather conditions are less than basic VFR weather minima). *Source: Jeppesen*
Speed Limit Area	Airspace of defined dimensions, independent from any other airspace area, where specific aircraft speed limits have been established by the appropriate Air Traffic Service (ATS) authority or Air Traffic Control (ATC) unit. *Source: Jeppesen*
Temporary Flight Restriction Area (TFR)	A TFR is a short-term airspace restriction in a limited geographical area, typically used in the United States. TFRs are generally established to restrict flight over major sporting events, natural disaster areas, air shows, space launches, and during Presidential movements. More information can be found in AIM Paragraph 3-5-3.

Temporary Reserve/ Segregated Areas (TRA)	A Temporary Reserved Area (TRA) is a defined volume of airspace normally under the jurisdiction of one aviation authority and temporarily reserved, by common agreement, for the specific use by another aviation authority and through which other traffic may be allowed to transit under an Air Traffic Service (ATS) authority. *Source: Excerpted from United Kingdom AIP*
Terminal Control Area (TCA/TMA)	A control area normally established at the confluence of Air Traffic Service (ATS) routes in the vicinity of one or more major aerodromes. *Source: ICAO International Civil Aviation Vocabulary* Note: In the United States, Class B airspace has replaced the term TCA.
Terminal Radar Service Area (TRSA)	Airspace surrounding designated airports wherein ATC provides radar vectoring, sequencing, and separation on a full-time basis for all IFR and participating VFR aircraft. The AIM contains an explanation of TRSA. TRSAs are depicted on VFR aeronautical charts. Pilot participation is urged but is not mandatory. *Source: AIM Pilot/Controller Glossary. See also AIM Paragraph 3-5-6*
Traffic Information Area/Zone (TIA/TIZ)	Traffic information areas (TIA) and traffic information zones (TIZ) are established at airports where the traffic is relatively light and therefore only Aerodrome Flight Information Service (AFIS) is provided. AFIS units do not issue clearances. The responsibility for avoiding collisions solely rests with the pilot when flying in to or out from these airports. The AFIS unit will state the runway in use, weather and traffic situation considered. *Source: ICAO International Civil Aviation Vocabulary*
Training Areas	Airspace of defined dimensions within which a high volume of pilot training or an unusual type of aerial activity may be carried out. *Source: Jeppesen*
Upper Control Area (UCA/UTA)	Controlled airspace established by an appropriate Air Traffic Service (ATS) authority or Air Traffic Control (ATC) unit, of defined dimensions and between upper altitude limits, which exists above terminal airspace area(s) where the terminal ATC unit also has responsibility for control of aircraft operating within the designated upper airspace. An Upper Control Area (UCA) is not associated with an airport. An Upper Terminal Area (UTA) is associated with an airport. *Source: Jeppesen*
Warning Areas	A warning area is airspace of defined dimensions extending from 3 nautical miles outward from the coast of the United States, that contains activity that may be hazardous to nonparticipating aircraft. The purpose of such warning area is to warn nonparticipating pilots of the potential danger. A warning area may be located over domestic or international waters or both. *Source: AIM Pilot/Controller Glossary (Special Use Airspace). See also AIM Paragraph 3-4-4*

Sources

- FAA *Federal Aviation Regulations/Aeronautical Information Manual.* Online at http://www.faa.gov/airports_airtraffic/air_traffic/publications/atpubs/aim/

- ICAO, *International Civil Aviation Vocabulary/Vocabulaire de l'aviation civile,* 2002

- NavCanada, *Canada Flight Supplement*
- Transport Canada, *Designated Airspace Handbook*. Issue No. 205, 31 July 2008. Online at http://www.navcanada.ca/ContentDefinitionFiles/Publications/AeronauticalInfoProducts/DAH/DAH_Next_EN.pdf
- Austria, *Aeronautical Information Publication*
- Islamic Republic of Iran, *Aeronautical Information Publication*
- Norway, *Aeronautical Information Publication*
- Japan, *Aeronautical Information Publication*
- United Kingdom, *Aeronautical Information Publication*
- Norway, *Aeronautical Information Circular* (AIC), June 2008. Online at https://www.ippc.no/ippc/display_pdf_or_url_servlet?origfilename=EN_Circ_2008_A_006_en.pdf

Appendix D: Detailed Results of Line Sorting Task

Each column in the following table indicates responses by several different pilot groups to one of the 65 items that were sorted. The following symbol codes are used:

⊕⊕⊕   Very Useful (statistically significant)
+   Not statistically significant, but the most common response was Very Useful
−   Not statistically significant, but the most common response was Do Not Use/Recognize
⇓   Do Not Use/Recognize (statistically significant)

Blank cells indicate either a mix of responses or cases where Somewhat Useful was the most common response. By scanning down the columns, it is possible to see which items were generally useful to all pilot groups, which were useful to a subset of pilot groups, and which were not useful, or not recognized, in general.

When a display is being developed to meet the needs of more than one of the pilot groups shown below, the designers should consider all of the potential system users, and include items on the display that are useful to any *one* of these groups individually. For example, systems developed for use by private operators (regardless of the purpose of the flight or whether it is conducted under IFR or VFR should combine the results from the relevant groups, e.g., Private IFR (P-IFR), Private VFR (P-VFR), and Private Business (P-Business).

Table 33. Line sorting results for items 1 through 10, ADIZ through Caution Area.

Item #	1	2	3	4	5	6	7	8	9	10
Item	Air Defense Identification Zones (ADIZ)	Air Route Traffic Control Center (ARTCC)	Airport Radar Service Area (ARSA)	Alert Areas (A)	Alternate, Conditional or Uncontrolled Enroute Airway or ATS Route	Altimeter Setting Regions (QFE/QNH)	Balloon Launch Area	Bluff	Buffer Zone/Non-Free Flying Zone	Caution Areas (C)
IFR Pilots	⊕⊕⊕	+	−	−	⇓	⇓	⇓	⇓	⇓	⇓
VFR Pilots	⊕⊕⊕	⇓	⇓	−	⇓	⇓	⇓	⇓	⇓	⇓
P-IFR	+	+	+	+	⇓	⇓	⇓	⇓	⇓	−
P-VFR	⊕⊕⊕	⇓	⇓	−	⇓	⇓	⇓	⇓	⇓	⇓
P-Business	⊕⊕⊕		−	+	⇓	−	⇓	⇓	⇓	−
Corporate	+			+	⇓	−	−	⇓	⇓	−
Air Transport		+	−	−	⇓	+	⇓	⇓	⇓	−
Military	+	+			−		−	−	⇓	+
International	+	+	⇓	−	⇓	+	⇓	⇓	⇓	−
FAA/Regulatory	+	+			−	−	−	−	−	−
Less than 1 hr		−	+	−	⇓	⇓	⇓	⇓	⇓	⇓
1-3 Hr	⊕⊕⊕	−	−	−	⇓	⇓	⇓	⇓	⇓	⇓
3-6 Hr	⊕⊕⊕	+	⇓	+	⇓	−	⇓	⇓	⇓	−
6+ Hr	+	+	−	−	−	+	−	⇓	⇓	−

Table 34. Line sorting results for items 11 through 20, City Pattern through Contour.

Item #	11	12	13	14	15	16	17	18	19	20
Item	City Pattern	Class A Airspace	Class B Airspace	Class C Airspace	Class D Airspace	Class E Airspace	Class F Airspace	Class G Airspace	CNS/ATM Equipment Requirement Areas (RNP, RVSM, MNPS, Mode C, etc.)	Contours
IFR Pilots	⇓	−	⊕⊕⊕	⊕⊕⊕	⊕⊕⊕	−	⇓	⇓	+	+
VFR Pilots	⊕⊕⊕	⇓	⊕⊕⊕	⊕⊕⊕	⊕⊕⊕	⊕⊕⊕	⇓	⇓	⇓	⊕⊕⊕
P-IFR		−	⊕⊕⊕	⊕⊕⊕	⊕⊕⊕	+	⇓	−	⇓	
P-VFR	⊕⊕⊕	⇓	⊕⊕⊕	⊕⊕⊕	⊕⊕⊕	⊕⊕⊕	⇓	⇓	⇓	⊕⊕⊕
P- Business	+	−	⊕⊕⊕	⊕⊕⊕	⊕⊕⊕	+	⇓	−	−	+
Corporate	+	−	⊕⊕⊕	⊕⊕⊕	⊕⊕⊕	+	⇓	+		+
Air Transport	⇓	+	+	⊕⊕⊕	+	−	⇓	⇓	⊕⊕⊕	+
Military	−	+	⊕⊕⊕	⊕⊕⊕	⊕⊕⊕		−		+	
International	⇓	+	+	⊕⊕⊕	+	−	⇓	⇓	⊕⊕⊕	+
FAA/Regulatory		+	⊕⊕⊕	⊕⊕⊕	+	+	−	−	+	
Less than 1 Hr	+	−	⊕⊕⊕	⊕⊕⊕	⊕⊕⊕	+	−	−	⇓	+
1-3 Hr	⊕⊕⊕	⇓	⊕⊕⊕	⊕⊕⊕	⊕⊕⊕	⊕⊕⊕	⇓	⇓	⇓	⊕⊕⊕
3-6 Hr	−	−	⊕⊕⊕	⊕⊕⊕	+	−	⇓	⇓	−	+
6+ Hr	−	+		⊕⊕⊕	+	+	−	−	⊕⊕⊕	+

Table 35. Line sorting results for items 21 through 30, Control Area through Helicopter Zone.

Item #	21	22	23	24	25	26	27	28	29	30
Item	Control Area (CTA/CTL)	Control Zone/Air Traffic Zone (CTR/CTZ/ATZ)	Controlled Firing Area (CFA) (United States)	Country (State) Boundary	Danger Areas (D)	Enroute Airway or ATS Route	Enroute ATC Holding Pattern	Flight Information Region/Upper Flight Information Region (FIR/UIR)	Formation Radial or Bearing (Enroute & Terminal)	Helicopter Traffic Zone/Protected Zone (HTZ/HPZ)
IFR Pilots	⇓	+	⇓	+	−	⊕⊕⊕	⊕⊕⊕	−	⇓	⇓
VFR Pilots	⇓	⇓	⇓	+	⇓	−	⇓	⇓	⇓	⇓
P-IFR	⇓	−	⇓	−	⇓	⊕⊕⊕		⇓	−	⇓
P-VFR	⇓	⇓	⇓	+	⇓	+	⇓	⇓	⇓	⇓
P- Business	⇓	+	⇓		−	+	−	⇓	⇓	⇓
Corporate	⇓	−	⇓	+	⇓	+		−	⇓	⇓
Air Transport	+	⊕⊕⊕	⇓	+	⊕⊕⊕	⊕⊕⊕	⊕⊕⊕	⊕⊕⊕	⇓	⇓
Military		−	−	+	−	⊕⊕⊕	+	+	−	⇓
International	+	⊕⊕⊕	⇓	+	⊕⊕⊕	⊕⊕⊕	+	⊕⊕⊕	⇓	⇓
FAA/Regulatory	+	+	−		−	⊕⊕⊕	+	+	+	−
Less than 1 Hr	⇓	−	⇓		⇓	−	⇓	⇓	⇓	⇓
1-3 Hr	⇓	⇓	⇓	+	⇓	⊕⊕⊕	⇓	⇓	⇓	⇓
3-6 Hr	−	+	⇓	+	+	⊕⊕⊕	+	+	⇓	⇓
6+ Hr	⊕⊕⊕	+	⇓	+	+	⊕⊕⊕	⊕⊕⊕	⊕⊕⊕	−	⇓

Table 36. Line sorting results for items 31 through 40, International Date Line through Positive Control Area.

Item #	31	32	33	34	35	36	37	38	39	40
Item	International Date Line	Isogonic Lines	Lake or Pond	Military Control Zone/Military Air Traffic Zone (MCTR/MATZ)	Military Operations Area (MOA)	Missed Approach Procedure Holding Pattern	Missed Approach Procedure Track	National Security Area (NSA) (United States)	Oceanic Control Area (OCA)	Positive Control Area (PCA)
IFR Pilots	⇓	⇓		⇓	+	⊕⊕⊕	⊕⊕⊕	⇓	⇓	⇓
VFR Pilots	⇓	–	⊕⊕⊕	⇓	⊕⊕⊕	⇓	⇓	⇓	⇓	⇓
P-IFR	⇓		+	⇓	⊕⊕⊕	⊕⊕⊕	⊕⊕⊕	–	⇓	–
P-VFR	⇓	–	⊕⊕⊕	⇓	⊕⊕⊕	⇓	⇓	⇓	⇓	⇓
P- Business	–	–	+	⇓	⊕⊕⊕	+	+	⇓	⇓	⇓
Corporate		–	⊕⊕⊕	⇓	⊕⊕⊕	⊕⊕⊕	+	–	–	–
Air Transport	⇓	⇓	–	⇓	–	⊕⊕⊕	⊕⊕⊕	⇓	+	⇓
Military	–	–		–	⊕⊕⊕	⊕⊕⊕	⊕⊕⊕	–	–	–
International	⇓	–	–	⇓	–	⊕⊕⊕	⊕⊕⊕	⇓	+	⇓
FAA/Regulatory					+	⊕⊕⊕	⊕⊕⊕	–		
Less than 1 Hr	⇓	–	⊕⊕⊕	⇓	⊕⊕⊕	⇓	⇓	⇓	⇓	⇓
1-3 Hr	⇓	⇓	⊕⊕⊕	⇓	⊕⊕⊕	⇓	⇓	⇓	⇓	⇓
3-6 Hr	⇓	–		–	+	⊕⊕⊕	⊕⊕⊕	⇓	–	⇓
6+ Hr	–	–	–	–	–	⊕⊕⊕	⊕⊕⊕	⇓	⊕⊕⊕	⇓

Table 37. Line sorting results for items 41 through 50, Prohibited Airspace through Speed Limit Area.

Item #	41	42	43	44	45	46	47	48	49	50
Item	Prohibited Airspace Area (P)	Radar Vector Track	Railroad (single or multiple track)	Restricted Airspace Area (R)	River or Stream	Road (single or multi-lane)	Shoreline	Special Rules Area/Zone (SRA/SRZ)	Special VFR NA (Fixed Wing) Airspace	Speed Limit Area
IFR Pilots	⊕⊕⊕	⇓	⇓	⊕⊕⊕	−	−	+	⇓	⇓	⇓
VFR Pilots	⊕⊕⊕	⇓	⊕⊕⊕	⊕⊕⊕	⊕⊕⊕	⊕⊕⊕	⊕⊕⊕	⇓	⇓	⇓
P-IFR	⊕⊕⊕	⇓		⊕⊕⊕	+	+	+	⇓	⇓	⇓
P-VFR	⊕⊕⊕	⇓	⊕⊕⊕	⊕⊕⊕	⊕⊕⊕	⊕⊕⊕	⊕⊕⊕	⇓	⇓	⇓
P- Business	⊕⊕⊕	⇓	+	⊕⊕⊕	+	+	+	⇓	⇓	⇓
Corporate	⊕⊕⊕	⇓	+	⊕⊕⊕	⊕⊕⊕	+	+	⇓	−	⇓
Air Transport	⊕⊕⊕	−	⇓	⊕⊕⊕	⇓	⇓		⇓	⇓	+
Military	⊕⊕⊕			⊕⊕⊕				−	−	−
International	⊕⊕⊕	⇓	⇓	⊕⊕⊕	⇓	⇓	−	⇓	⇓	+
FAA/Regulatory	+			+				−	−	
Less than 1 Hr	⊕⊕⊕	⇓	⊕⊕⊕	⊕⊕⊕	⊕⊕⊕	⊕⊕⊕	+	⇓	⇓	⇓
1-3 Hr	⊕⊕⊕	⇓	⊕⊕⊕	⊕⊕⊕	⊕⊕⊕	⊕⊕⊕	⊕⊕⊕	⇓	⇓	⇓
3-6 Hr	⊕⊕⊕	⇓	⇓	⊕⊕⊕	−	−		⇓	⇓	−
6+ Hr	⊕⊕⊕	−	⇓	+	−	⇓	−	⇓	⇓	+

Table 38. Line sorting results for items 31 through 40, International Date Line through Positive Control Area.

Item #	51	52	53	54	55	56	57	58	59	60
Item	Telephone or Power Lines	Temporary Flight Restriction Area (TFR)	Temporary Reserve/Segregated Areas (European equivalent of MOA)	Terminal ATC Holding Pattern	Terminal Control Area (TCA/TMA)	Terminal Procedure Course Reversal Holding Pattern	Terminal Procedure Flight Track	Terminal Radar Service Area (TRSA)	Terminal Transition or Feeder Route (Arrival, Departure, Approach)	Time Zone Boundary
IFR Pilots	⇓	−	⇓	⊕⊕⊕	⊕⊕⊕	−	⊕⊕⊕	−	⊕⊕⊕	−
VFR Pilots	⊕⊕⊕	⊕⊕⊕	⇓	⇓	⇓	⇓	⇓	+	⇓	⇓
P-IFR		⊕⊕⊕	⇓	+	−	+	−	+	+	
P-VFR	⊕⊕⊕	⊕⊕⊕	⇓	⇓	⇓	⇓	⇓	+	⇓	⇓
P- Business	−	⊕⊕⊕	⇓	+	+	−	−	−	−	
Corporate	+	⊕⊕⊕	⇓	+	+	+			−	
Air Transport	⇓	⇓	⇓	⊕⊕⊕	⊕⊕⊕	+	⊕⊕⊕	−	⊕⊕⊕	−
Military	−	+	⇓	+	−	+	⊕⊕⊕		⊕⊕⊕	−
International	⇓	⇓	⇓	⊕⊕⊕	⊕⊕⊕	−	⊕⊕⊕	−	⊕⊕⊕	−
FAA/Regulatory		+	−	⊕⊕⊕	+	−	+		⊕⊕⊕	
Less than 1 Hr	+	⊕⊕⊕	⇓	⇓	+	⇓	⇓	+	⇓	⇓
1-3 Hr	⊕⊕⊕	⊕⊕⊕	⇓	⇓	⇓	⇓	⇓	+	⇓	⇓
3-6 Hr	⇓	−	⇓	+	+	−	+	−	+	
6+ Hr	⇓	−	⇓	+	⊕⊕⊕		+	+	⊕⊕⊕	−

Table 39. Line sorting results for items 61 through 65, Traffic Information Area/Zone through Warning Area.

Item #	61	62	63	64	65
Item	Traffic Information Area/Zone (TIA/TIZ)	Training Areas (T)	Upper Control Area (UCA/UTA)	Visual Flight Track	Warning Area (W)
IFR Pilots	⇓	⇓	⇓	⇓	⊕⊕⊕
VFR Pilots	⇓	⇓	⇓	⇓	+
P-IFR	⇓	⇓	⇓	⇓	+
P-VFR	⇓	⇓	⇓	⇓	⊕⊕⊕
P- Business	⇓	⇓	⇓	−	+
Corporate	⇓	⇓	⇓	−	
Air Transport	⇓	⇓	−	−	+
Military	⇓	−	−	−	⊕⊕⊕
International	⇓	⇓	−	−	⊕⊕⊕
FAA/Regulatory	−		−	+	+
Less than 1 Hr	⇓	−	⇓	⇓	−
1-3 Hr	⇓	⇓	⇓	⇓	⊕⊕⊕
3-6 Hr	⇓	⇓	⇓	−	⊕⊕⊕
6+ Hr	−	−	⊕⊕⊕	−	+

www.ingramcontent.com/pod-product-compliance
Lightning Source LLC
Chambersburg PA
CBHW070304290526
45791CB00003B/1075